ACTION ON THE STREETS

A Handbook for
Inner City Youth Work

ACTION

A Handbook for Inner City Youth Work

ASSOCIATION PRESS

ON THE STREETS

FRANK J. CARNEY
HANS W. MATTICK
JOHN D. CALLAWAY

NEW YORK

ACTION ON THE STREETS: A HANDBOOK FOR INNER CITY YOUTH WORK

Association Press, 291 Broadway, New York, N.Y. 10007

SBN Cloth: 8096-1715-3

Paperback: 8096-1721-8

Library of Congress catalog card number: 69-18837

 72

Printed in the United States of America

Portions of three chapters in this book include material from: Hans W.
Mattick and Nathan S. Caplan, "Stake Animals, Loud Talking and Leadership
in Do-Nothing and Do-Something Situations" in *Juvenile Gangs in Context:
Theory, Research and Action*, Malcolm W. Klein and Barbara G. Myerhoff, eds.,
© 1967. By permission of Prentice-Hall, Inc., Englewood Cliffs, New Jersey.

Acknowledgments

THE experience and insight reflected in this manual of out-reach work with youth is not only that of its three authors. We would be remiss if we did not give credit where credit is due by identifying the workers and supervisors of the CYDP from whom we learned so much:

Earl F. Doty, Associate Director of Community Organization
Nathan S. Caplan, Associate Director of Research
Gerald D. Suttles, Research Assistant
Daniel R. Scheinfeld, Research Assistant
Dennis J. Deshaies, Research Assistant
John L. Ray, Outpost Supervisor
Warner Saunders, Street-Club Worker
Levert P. King, Street-Club Worker
Antonio Irizarry, Street-Club Worker
Ezra Smith, Street-Club Worker
Fred W. Christie, Street-Club Worker
Eugene Perkins, Street-Club Worker
Richard M. Booze, Street-Club Worker
James E. Maryland, Street-Club Worker
Martin E. Dann, Street-Club Worker
Flint Anderson, Street-Club Worker
Christiel Davis, Girls' Street-Club Worker
Solon M. Ice, Community Organizer
Norman B. Weiss, Community Organizer
Ronald J. Wolsfeld, Community Organizer
Lincoln A. Blakeney, Club Director
Oscar F. Hartman, Club Director
Obern Simons, Program Director
Jeff Underwood, Program Director
Martin Gold, Research Program Director

Introduction

THE experience and practice reflected in this manual is that
of the Chicago Youth Development Project (CYDP), the largest
privately-financed delinquency prevention and control project ever
conducted in the City of Chicago. During its six-year life span,
from July 1, 1960 to June 30, 1966, some eighty persons staffed its
action and research programs, and more than 5,000 persons, youth
and adult, were affected, in one way or another, by its multifarious
activities. Although thus located in space and time, its methods
and experience have a wide range of applicability to a large variety
of public and private agencies located in towns, cities or suburbs
across the nation. Any agency that is engaged in "out-reach work
with youth," or plans to develop such a program, will find this
recorded experience of its predecessors a useful source of information and training materials as it seeks to come to grips with the
burgeoning youth problem of our era. Those who will not learn
from history are doomed to repeat it. This experience and practice
manual was written in order to enable our successors to profit from
our knowledge so that they may surpass us in their efforts.

The CYDP was a joint project of the Chicago Boys' Clubs and
the Institute for Social Research of The University of Michigan.
It was financed by grants from the Ford Foundation ($1,225,000)
and the W. Clement and Jessie V. Stone Foundation ($174,000),
with about two-thirds of the money going to the action program
and the remaining third being spent on research and evaluation.
Although many persons in Chicago and Ann Arbor played an active
role in the conduct of this project, the experience and practice reflected in the text is mainly that of the street-club workers and
community organizers who carried out the out-reach action program
that is the heart of the project.

7

Although there was a good deal of joint planning and interaction between the action and research teams of the CYDP, there was a definite division of labor between them. The action out-reach program was organized and implemented by the Chicago Boys' Clubs and, more particularly, by the CYDP staffs of the two boys clubs units (the Henry Horner Chicago Boys' Club and the Oldtown Chicago Boys' Club) located in the inner city areas where the project was conducted. The research design and evaluative program was planned and carried out by the Institute for Social Research and, more particularly, by a special research team based in Chicago.

The action out-reach program of the CYDP consisted of a three-fold attack on the problem of delinquency: (1) street-club work with young people, (2) community organization work with local adults, and (3) the use of informal facilities. The first was called the Extension Work program and consisted, essentially, of having street-club workers come into contact with young people wherever they might congregate in the action area, bringing them under the influence and supervision of the workers and attempting to deal constructively with the significant problems in their lives that might be amenable to intervention. We found that youth were not "hard-to-reach," they were only hard to work with after they *had* been reached. The second was the Community Organization program and consisted, essentially, of organizing local adults, agencies and resources around problem youngsters or local conditions with a view to resolving the problematic situation concerned. We found many persons in the local community who were willing to help if the problem involved could be clearly communicated. The third was the Outpost program and consisted, essentially, of providing informal facilities like store fronts, garages or basement rooms of public housing buildings, where the CYDP staff and the youngsters with whom they were working could be brought together under continuous and optimum counseling conditions. We found that the youngsters, and especially the older teen-agers, preferred such facilities to the more formal atmosphere of a boys' club or the traditional youth-serving agency. And it must be remembered, from the standpoint of providing informal facilities, a car or a station wagon is simply a mobile counseling room with a great attraction for young people.[1]

The five general areas of theoretical and practical interest which shaped the methods and goals of the CYDP were: (1) the inadequate conventional socialization of the young; (2) the lack of legitimate opportunity for the young, especially minority group members; (3) the alienation of youth from adults and the lack of consensus about conventional values; (4) the disorganization of family and community life under the impact of urbanization in the inner city; and (5) the latent negative effects of handling youthful offenders through formal legal channels and institutions. The action program of the CYDP was designed to effect some positive changes in those aspects of these five problem areas that expressed themselves in the form of antisocial behavior and juvenile delinquency.

The action out-reach goals of the CYDP were:

1. To reduce the absolute amount of illegal and antisocial behavior attributable to the target population in the experimental areas.

2. To change the behavior of individuals and groups in the contacted part of the target population, where necessary, from the more seriously antisocial to the less seriously, and from the less seriously antisocial to the conventional, within the class and cultural norms of the local population.

3. To help individuals and groups in the contacted part of the target population meet their emotional needs for association, friendship and status by providing conventional, organized and supervised activities for them, with a view to increasing their capacity for participation and autonomy.

4. To increase the objective opportunities for youth in the external environment, in the field of education, employment and cultural experiences.

5. To help youth prepare themselves for conventional adult roles by providing guidance in the fields of education, work, family life and citizenship through direct intervention in their life processes, especially at times of crisis.

6. To relate the target population to local adults and institutions

in positive ways so that communication channels between youth and adults may be developed through which a shared, conventional system of values may be transmitted.

7. To develop in parents and local adults a concern for local problems affecting youth welfare, and to organize them with a view to having them assume responsibility for the resolution of local problems.

8. To create a positive change in attitude, in both youth and adults, about the possibility of local self-help efforts to improve the local community through active and cooperative intervention in community processes, and thus create a more positive attitude toward the local community itself.

The CYDP staff that conducted the action out-reach program designed to achieve these goals, and the research team that evaluated this effort, were organized into the following structure:

Chicago Boys Club   *Institute for Social Research*

CYDP Director, ISR & CBC

Associate Director—Street Work, CBC
Associate Director—Community Organization, CBC
Associate Director–Research, ISR
(Secretarial and Clerical Staff)

Area I-X	Area II-X	Research
(Horner), CBC	(Oldtown), CBC	Team, ISR
Club Director	Club Director	Program Director
Program Director	Program Director	Asst. Program Dir.
4 Street-Club Workers	2 Street-Club Workers	3 Research Asst., Chgo.
2 Community Organizers	1 Community Organizer	Sampling Consultant
1 Secretary-Clerk	1 Secretary-Clerk	Sec'y-Clerical support

Action area I-X (Horner) consisted of ten census tracts comprising a one-mile-square area. It was bounded by streets located 400 north, 400 south, 1600 west and 2400 west in Chicago's street-numbering grid pattern. According to the 1960 census, this area had a total population of 30,269 persons, 81.5% of whom were non-white and 7.2% of whom were males aged 10 to 19—the target population of the CYDP. Area II-X (Oldtown) consisted of six census tracts and was slightly more than one-half-mile square in area. It was bounded by streets located at 500 south, 1200 south, 1000 west and 1600 west. It had a total population of 20,524 persons, 17.3% of whom were non-white and 8.6% of whom were males aged 10 to 19. Combined, these areas had a total population of 50,793 persons, 3,926 of whom were males aged 10 to 19, whose behavior and life-chances the CYDP action out-reach staff and program hoped to affect in a positive manner.

At any one time, once the project was fully staffed and organized, in an average month, the action staff of the CYDP had some form of contact or association with about 1,500 youngsters and 1,200 local adults in the regular course of their work. In terms of organized groups, however, with whom the CYDP were in almost daily interaction, there were, on the average, about forty street gangs and the same number of adult community organizations and agencies. These organized gangs had a total core membership of 470 individuals (approximately 20% were female groups or hangers-on), and the adult organizations had about 780 active members (approximately 50% were males).

The organization and planning of the CYDP provided for extensive and frequent record-keeping procedures in order to gain the benefits of written records and to reduce the human distortions of fallible memories. Contact cards were made out for every youngster and adult contacted by the workers. Every street-club worker and community organizer wrote a Daily Activity Report of his day's experience as a regular part of his work. The Program Directors of the two participating boys' clubs submitted bi-monthly summary reports on CYDP workers and their activities. Both Club Directors and all three Associate Directors of the CYDP wrote monthly summary reports. The three Research Assistants wrote Daily Activity Reports the first two years of the project, before they got involved in extensive survey and evaluative research activities. By special agreement with the Chicago Police Department Youth Division, every youngster arrested and not detained in custody, who lived in the action areas, was referred to the CYDP for a follow-up home visit.

The result of all this record-keeping was the systematic accumulation of: 7,000 contact cards, 12,000 daily activities reports, 350 supervisory and research reports, and 2,250 arrest cards on juveniles. Altogether, these records constituted an excellent running history of CYDP staff and client activities, a description of gross and minor changes in the action areas, a reflection of the changes in the nature of the population contacted by the staff, and a complete history of the incidence of arrest and recidivism among juveniles resident in the action areas during the last three years of the project. Although the research team was able to make use of these records, their main function was largely that of administrative and supervisory control over the action program. The research team devised its own separate research instruments, questionnaires and archival records relating to arrests, school drop-out rates, youth employment, gang membership and action staff relations with youngsters.

The foregoing would not have been detailed at such length if it were not the introduction to a point of central importance in outreach work with youth. This stress on record-keeping is intended to convey the seriousness of purpose, the high degree of administrative and supervisory control, and the deep need of accurate and systematic knowledge that dominated the CYDP action staff and program. Most of the traditional youth-serving agencies, both public and private, maintain only the most elementary and transient records related to narrowly conceived functional needs. The result is that they have only the vaguest notions about the nature of their own work and its effects, if any, on the youngsters who are their client population. The main danger in the failure to keep systematic records is that of being led astray by individual and dramatic cases of success or failure that form the basis of poor generalizations. Thus the social reality of youth out-reach work is easily lost and the groundwork is laid for manufacturing a mythology that complicates and aggravates the very problem with which it is seeking to come to grips. More frequently than not, these myths serve public relations and fund-raising purposes rather than promoting an understanding of the reality situation of inner city youth.

No youth-serving agency, public or private, can afford to engage in myth-making operations by putting forward exaggerated claims or images, positive or negative, without alienating their youthful clients and making their own work more difficult in the long run.

The traditional youth-serving agency, or other bureaucracies, public and private, that relate themselves to youth, have to make up their mind whether they want to live off of the fact that youth have problems, or whether they want to deal with these problems in a constructive way. If, for purposes of fund-raising, empire-building or public-relations imagery, a public or private youth-serving agency portrays youth as a dangerous, slavering beast—a knife-wielding, chain-swinging, over-sexed, drug-using monster—from whom the community can best be protected by that agency's special expertise and mystique, then the youth problem has been compounded. This is the imagery of the short-sighted public-relations department that has its eye on the dollar rather than on the real task of the agency, which is to help train and assimilate youngsters into the conventional social structure. It is easy to frighten middle-class donors, or taxpayers, or to appeal to their sense of guilt, in the course of a fund-raising campaign; but when the campaign is over, very few of these middle-class types can be persuaded to teach, employ or otherwise associate with such "beasts." Yet, what the youth-serving agency really needs is the ability to provide educational and employment opportunities to youth, and to bring youth into fruitful association with adults whom they can respect. No amount of "conscience and fright money" can create such conventional opportunities for youth. It is really much better for the youth-serving agency to portray their work with youth in a realistic and honest fashion; to simply tell the truth, the good with the bad and vice versa.

Many, if not most, of the claims and assertions made by the specialized bureaucratic hierarchies that relate themselves to, and report upon the activities of, inner city youth strike the experienced out-reach worker at the street level as being simply ludicrous.[2] This is true whether the assertions being made are the stereotypes of the mass media, the occupationally-structured perceptions of the school, welfare or police authorities, or the selective and dramatic cases so beloved of the traditional youth-serving agency engaged in public relations. It is not that these bureaucracies and occupational groups are dishonest; they are simply the "victims" of inadequate and structurally-biased reporting practices—a very human failing. The kind of thing that happens is this: (1) the worker at the lowest level (the street-club worker, the schoolteacher, the case-welfare worker, the patrolman or the news reporter) reports the "mess of reality" as it is reflected in his street-level perception of the situations he is obliged to deal with; (2) his supervisor (the club director, the school principal, the supervising social worker, the police captain or the copy editor), however, either cannot use, or does not want to hear about, this "mess of reality." He has problems of his own—too much work, not enough manpower, the exigencies of a busy life—which require a different view of reality. He wants to be helpful, but there are limitations on his time and energy that he communicates to the levels above and below him. Thus, at this second level, a "clean-up" process of selection, rationalization and ordering of priorities begins. (3) When the first-level supervisor reports on his work to his supervisor (the executive director of several youth-serving agency units, the district school superintendent, the head of the branch welfare office, the police commissioner or the city editor), the selective process of communication has, again, refined the "cleaned-up mess of reality"; it is now simpler, more general, and beginning to take on the logical, conceptual form of processed information structured by the internal needs of a bureaucratic hierarchy. (4) By the time that the top level of the organization (the board of trustees of the youth-serving agency, the board of education, the city welfare board, the mayor's office or the newspaper publisher) receives what is left of the original street-level perception of the "mess of reality," it has undergone a remarkable transformation: the youth-serving agency has had a "high degree of success," the school system has been "educating" the youth, the welfare system has been "adequately serving" its clients, the city administration has been "coping" with crime and disorder, and the mass media have reported "accurately" on the nature of reality. Unfortunately, these refined versions of reality are not reflected in the work and experience of the lowest-level worker, who is obliged to confront the same old "mess of reality" and do what he can to bring order out of chaos while seeking the support and help of those above him who have their own version of reality.

How one avoids, or corrects for, the shortcomings of such a selective communication process that tends to mislead us all, is a difficult question. At least two suggestions can be made from the experience of the CYDP: (1) the reduction of day-to-day experience to writing and the maintenance of systematically kept records is not only a great corrective for a faulty memory and the mythology that grows out of individual, selected, dramatic cases (good or bad), but it tends toward the prevention of making poor generalizations and the construction of false stereotypes; (2) supervision procedures must be devised and practiced that link the top and the bottom levels of a bureaucratic hierarchy so that the top level is not "victimized" by the selective communication process that has been described. The image of Plato's philosopher-king descending into the cave again, or Mayor Lindsay of New York walking the streets of Harlem and talking to the people, comes readily to mind. The supervision processes of the CYDP "short-circuited" its own bureaucratic and hierarchical structure in the interest of gaining the fullest understanding possible of the youth situation in the areas where the project was conducted. Both the Associate Director of Street Work and the Associate Director of Community Organization were in the field every day, from 2:00 P.M. to 10:00 P.M., and the Project Director spent two or three evenings of every week in the field talking to all the workers and many of the young people with whom they were working. There was very little that went on in the action areas of the CYDP that was not known, personally and directly, by all levels of the field staff and their supervisors. The CYDP was far from a perfect project, but it suffered from far fewer delusions of reality than the traditional youth-serving agency or many of the bureaucracies that deal with youth.

In the end, the question must be faced: did the CYDP "succeed" in preventing juvenile delinquency, or in achieving its other goals? This is not a simple question with a simple answer, for much depends upon what is meant by "success." From one point of view it would be simple to produce a positive, but partial, answer that would give the appearance of success. For example, during its six-year life span the CYDP staff succeeded in finding 750 jobs for 490 young people; similarly, 950 school drop-outs were returned to school 1,400 times. CYDP out-reach workers made 1,250 appearances at police stations and courts on behalf of 800 youngsters and, in part because of their intervention, the police and courts were willing to dispose of such cases by station adjustments or probation. Finally, CYDP workers made 2,700 follow-up visits to the homes of 2,000 juveniles who were arrested during the last thirty months of the project, in an effort to get them involved in one aspect or another of the project's programs. All of these figures reveal a deeply committed, well-related and task-oriented staff that was doing its job, and doing it well. Insofar as youth employment, school attendance, community supervision over offenders and contact with youth known to the police are indices of success, the CYDP succeeded to a remarkable degree. There is no doubt that most of the young people indicated by these statistics were helped in a constructive way through the efforts of the CYDP. In addition, hundreds of others were helped and influenced in a variety of ways through the counseling and guidance extended by the CYDP out-reach workers in their day-to-day association with young people. There is just no way to measure the longer range, "sleeper" effects of out-reach work, *i.e.*, the sense in which an older worker has a constructive influence on a young boy that does not become manifest until that younger boy begins to mature.

There is another way, however, of raising the question of the meaning of "success" in out-reach work, and that is to ask whether the CYDP had any effects on the *rate* of youth employment, on the school drop-out *rate*, or on the *rates* of arrest and conviction of young people who got into trouble. At first blush it would appear to be "obvious" that such a busy project as the CYDP must have had some positive effects on these rates; but the fact is that it did not. Despite the successful efforts of the staff in finding jobs, returning school drop-outs and intervening in formal legal processes, the youth unemployment rate remained at about the same level, the school drop-out rate increased slightly and the arrest rates of youngsters in the CYDP areas increased over time, with a lesser proportion of them being disposed of as station adjustments.

Here we have what seems to be a strange contradiction: the CYDP helped many individual youngsters, but the project failed to achieve its goals. How could that be? The explanation seemed to be that CYDP out-reach workers were very good at achieving "most-favored client" relations for the youngsters with whom they happened to be working. Thus, for example, a worker could bring a drop-out to a school counselor and convince the school authorities that they should re-admit this student. The authorities would agree on condition that the worker would support the motivation of the student and help him with his homework and other problems. More frequently than not, this procedure would work and the school drop-out would have been successfully returned to school. At the same time, however, some other youngster, not known or related to any part of the CYDP project, would have dropped out of school or gotten himself expelled and the school drop-out rate would remain static. Thus, despite the expenditure of time, effort and money, the basic situation remained largely the same.

No matter how the research team measured it, there were "no significant differences," as the social scientists put it, in the basic forces that tended to produce delinquency. Although CYDP workers could find work for a series of individuals, they could not expand the absolute number of jobs available in the job market; although they could return drop-outs to school, they could not influence the behavior of youngsters and school administrators in such a way as to increase the rate of school attendance; and, although they could intervene between the youngsters and the police and courts, they could not prevent the rate of arrest from increasing. Apparently, the development of a whole series of "most-favored client" relationships with employers, the schools and the police on behalf of youngsters was not sufficient to overcome the systemic production of delinquency and its symptomatic correlates. On balance, and in the final analysis, the "experimental" population resident in the action areas of the CYDP seemed to be slightly worse off than the "control" population resident in a similar area selected for comparative purposes. This is *not* an unusual result in projects that are *adequately* researched *on their merits*.[3] But if the "successes" detailed above could only be claimed in a qualified way by the CYDP, neither could the "failures" be attributed to the project in an unqualified way. The relationship between the CYDP, its clients, its successes and failures, are complex, and still in the process of being sorted out by members of the research team at the Institute for

Social Research at The University of Michigan, but we already know the central thrust of the evaluation.

Apparently, the expenditure of $1,399,000 over a six-year period, the organization of a street-work and community organization project with a well-qualified and dedicated staff, operating in a mile-and-a-half-square area of an inner city, with a population base of 50,000 persons, including nearly 4,000 males aged 10 to 19 whose behavior is to be influenced in constructive ways, and a sustained and sophisticated effort to achieve this objective, can do a lot of good for many individuals who are touched by the project. If that is your main objective, out-reach work has the potential for achieving it. But, if you are mainly interested in dealing with the *problems* that contribute to delinquency: family disorganization, job opportunities, education, housing, discrimination, political representation and the negative impact of urbanization and large institutions on the lives of young people, then something more fundamental is required. Out-reach work has an important role to play, either as a stop-gap measure or as an essential element in a more fundamental program of social reform, but its strengths and weaknesses must be well understood. This experience and practice manual of out-reach work with youth is a contribution toward such understanding.

HANS W. MATTICK

FOOTNOTES

1 For a fuller description see: Hans W. Mattick and Nathan S. Caplan, *The Chicago Youth Development Project: A Descriptive Account of Its Action Program and Research Design*, Institute for Social Research, The University of Michigan, Ann Arbor, 1964.

2 See Walter B. Miller, "Violent Crimes in City Gangs," *The Annals of the American Academy of Political and Social Science*, Vol. 364, March, 1966.

3 See Edwin Powers and Helen Witmer, *An Experiment in the Prevention of Juvenile Delinquency: The Cambridge-Somerville Youth Study*, Columbia University Press, New York, 1951; Walter B. Miller, "The Impact of a 'Total-Community' Delinquency Control Project," *Social Problems*, Vol. 10, No. 2, Fall 1962; and James C. Hackler, "Boys, Blisters and Behavior: The Impact of a Work Program in an Urban Central Area," *Journal of Research in Crime and Delinquency*, July, 1966.

Contents

Alienation or Rapport:
To Be or Not To Be
"One of the Boys"

THE primary function of an out-reach worker is to establish and maintain some kind of a relationship between himself and youths who are his clients. Without such a relationship there can be no influence over the behavior of youngsters. What this means in practice is that, quite apart from the personal characteristics of youth—whether they are actually engaged in delinquent behavior or are merely perceived by the community as potentially delinquent—the out-reach worker must associate with them and know them or there is no basis for communication or control. An out-reach worker does not have to like a youth in order to have a reason for working with him, nor does the fact of working with a youth or a group imply approval of the entire range of behavior that such a youth or group may exhibit. As a matter of fact, it is probable that the youths who are most likeable and acceptable to out-reach workers are those who need his services least. Out-reach workers who invest their time and energy in only those youths who are likeable and ingratiating are apt to be seriously misled about the nature and seriousness of youth problems in the local community because their selection procedures have resulted in a biased reflection of the local youth situation. It is, therefore, important that out-reach workers reconcile themselves to the fact that they must work with some of the least likeable youngsters in an area.

An important question therefore arises. To what degree must an out-reach worker be like the youths with whom he works; what characteristics must they have in common and in what respects must they be different if the worker is to have some degree of influence over the behavior of his clients? If a worker's primary function is to establish and maintain relationships with youth, it is clear that there must be

21

some degree of rapport to sustain the relationship. The real question is one of similarities and differences, and where do you draw the line?

So much about our appearance, speech and conduct is symbolic that the way we look, talk and behave is quite as important a form of communication as the substance of what we say. Workers must, therefore, be self-conscious about the appearance they present, that is, their manner of dress and habits of personal grooming; they must be aware of the form and content of the language they use; and they must be mindful of the fact that their clients are a constant audience to their behavior. In general, the worker must manage himself in such a manner as to maintain rapport and not alienate the boys with whom he would be related, but he must achieve sufficient social distance and objectivity to enable him to communicate those things about himself that make him a model of pro-social behavior and influence. It is this line that is difficult to draw; but it must be drawn within the terms and conditions of maintaining relations between workers and boys.

In the matter of dress and personal grooming, CYDP out-reach workers dressed, according to season, in a manner befitting an acceptable and achievable model. They dressed neatly, including ties and sport coats in the winter and open-necked sport shirts and slacks in the summer. For all practical purposes they dressed very much like white-collar workers, with some degree of informality. For the most part, there was a clear difference between how the workers and their clients dressed, but the difference was not of such a magnitude that the clients could not imitate the workers' manner of dress with a little effort of up-grading and cleanliness. And, as a matter of fact, that is what happened in process of time on the part of boys who were responsive to the workers' efforts.

As regards language, the workers' speech was informal, making use of some slang that came naturally, but there was no deliberate attempt to imitate the "far-out jive" of some of the "cooler cats," or the dialect of recent rural migrants, except in the form of language games or parodies. There was some swearing when it seemed to be required for emphasis, but no obscenity for the sake of obscenity. At the same time there was an acute awareness of what might be called class-linked language styles, e.g., boys from a slum community are seldom "ill or injured," they are "sick and hurt"; similarly, they do not "soil their trousers," they "get their pants dirty." On the other hand, if the class-linked language style resulted in grammatical errors, e.g., "I is," then considerable effort was made to correct this, but always through humor and indirection.

Finally, as regards the general behavior of the worker, he was always aware that he served as an example or a model to boys who were observing him and passing judgment on his conduct. He always displayed good manners and politeness, despite an air of informality. He made no promises that he could not keep and kept those that he made. He always acted as if he expected his clients to keep their promises, although he anticipated some disappointments in this respect. He always respected confidences and acted as if he expected the boys with whom he worked to respect them. While he seemed to tolerate a wider latitude in obstreperous behavior, especially in the early stages of a relationship with a boy or a group, he did not compromise his own behavior, and he asserted standards for minimum conformity as soon as the strength of his relationship permitted him to do so. He accepted no gifts of material value and often refused to accept confidences of guilty knowledge that he could not communicate to others. In short, the out-reach workers of the CYDP were not members of a delinquent sub-culture, nor did they pretend to sympathize with delinquent values or conduct. The workers tended to view themselves as professional group workers working with youth and that is how they acted most of the time. They did not put on a "phony" sympathy act and did not allow themselves to be out-played and out-maneuvered by a few of their more delinquently clever clients. There were some points on which workers could be, and were, "sticklers," and some of these have been touched upon above.

On the other hand, some of the CYDP workers entered into relatively close personal relations with some of the youths and groups with whom they worked. The workers shared certain aspects of their own family life with their clients by bringing their children to the Outpost or some neighborhood affair. Similarly, on occasion the workers would take some of the group members to their homes or neighborhoods in order to demonstrate, by implication, the degree of friendliness, confidence and trust they had in their clients. This was not, however, a routine or expected work procedure for workers in the CYDP; it was, rather, a matter of personal choice and work style.

Altogether, the nature of the relationship that the out-reach workers of the CYDP were able to establish and maintain were such that the groups, on the whole, perceived our workers as being friendly, cheerful and generous. The youngsters seldom tested the workers' tolerance limits by provocative behavior and when they did the workers would respond by inquiring why they were being provoked rather than responding to the provocation itself. Such behavior on the part of the workers tended to disarm the youngsters and gained the concession that these workers were pretty "cool." In the parlance of the streets, such an endorsement of the worker is the badge of acceptance and rapport.

How the Out-Reach Worker
Makes Initial Contact

ONE of the most serious obstacles to effective out-reach work can be found in the imagination of the uninitiated worker. Very often the first question a worker is asked by someone interested in his work is, "How do you establish contact?" This question sometimes reflects an assumption on the questioner's part that establishing contact must be a difficult technique. He may have visions of the worker being required to "hang" on a street corner observing a group for several days or weeks before breaking the ice and making contact. This inhibition is rather common because while most of us can assume that people want and need contact with others we may also assume that threat is inherent in every human contact. For example, cub reporters who face their first interview with a famous personality usually feel intimidated. And parents meeting the teacher of their child frequently come to a first meeting with the authority-figure teacher very much on guard.)

Thus, with the images of street gangs fostered by the mass media and other romantics, the novice worker may come to assume that he will be dealing exclusively with a strange breed of tough, street-wise, antisocial, potentially violent youngsters.

This image, like most popular myths, has enough truth in it to be exploited or misrepresented by a variety of observers and, to some degree, by the youngsters themselves. Groups of youngsters observed on the streets are judged by their external appearance and other superficial criteria. If youngsters seem to fit a stereotype of "what a gang looks like," we must remember that inferences drawn from a stereotype frequently tell us as much about the observer as they do about the observed. Certain appearances, clothing styles, language habits and even physical stances reflect not only the local conformity patterns of youngsters, within their economic means, but also have a certain "survival value" indicating what it is that youngsters think they must do or be in order to "get by" in the neighborhood.

In the history of our project we experienced few cases in which a group refused to have anything to do with a worker who approached the group openly, explained who he was and what his purpose was. This is not to say that he was greeted with open arms at once but, with a little persistence and continuity of presenting himself for what he was, he managed to bridge the unknown. *Candor* is the first order of business in making contact with either a single member of a group or with the entire group.

We operated on the assumption that new contacts are threatening only when the motives of the newly contacted person and his perception of the contactor are ambiguous, hostile or deviant. But openness alone is not enough. Not only may youngsters feel threatened by a new contact with a "stranger," but the worker himself may feel uneasy about what he is getting into with this group. Therefore, some self-conscious procedures have to be gone through in order to reduce the tensions arising from these potential "threats." A good worker, we found, does his "homework" before contacting a new group. He knows what to look for, what to expect. But you might ask, "How does he know if he hasn't met the group before?"

The group is more or less known to others in the community. Our workers made it their regular business to solicit information from youth-serving agency people, teachers, juvenile officers of the police department, community leaders, parents and other youth. We were able to obtain from these sources different perceptions about the name of the group, where they congregated, the size of the group, the age range, the ethnicity, the employment picture, the past history of antisocial behavior and previous contact with youth-serving agencies.

At the same time, we did not fail to evaluate the sources of our information about street groups. Some observers have more opportunities than others to make observations. Other persons are simply in the local "rumor chain" and may know little more than the superficial gossip that contributes to the public mythology about gangs. Further, some informants or observers who are consulted about street groups may be biased by their occupation or some special relation they have to such groups, so all information must be carefully weighed and evaluated. If our experience counts for anything, it was our finding that "the truth" about street gangs lay somewhere between all the special views that observers had.

Probably the richest source of information about youth groups out on the street was other young people our workers had already contacted. Our workers quietly and consistently encouraged youngsters to talk about the groups they knew who were not in contact with us yet. The word-of-mouth "grapevine" is a constant source of contact information. But this information, too, must be carefully evaluated in the worker's mind because youngsters are as prone as others to give currency to the public mythology about street groups that serves many purposes. At best, what the new worker can learn about uncontacted street groups is an approximation of somewhat conflicting perspectives that tell him as much about his informants as they do about the group about whom he is seeking information. Nevertheless, the process of inquiry is necessary and instructive.

But even if a worker has had an opportunity to learn only a very little about a street group before contacting them for the first time, our experience indicates that his prospects for a successful contact are still good. Here are some helpful hints about how contact can be made:

Pick a time to approach the group when nothing much is going on so that you can be the focus of attention. Walk right in and stop in such a position so as to be heard speaking (in a normal tone of voice) to as many kids as possible. What you will say will, of course, depend on the facts, but it could be something like this:

"Hi. My name is Ralph Smith and I work for the Boys' Club. I'm new in the area and I'm going around trying to get acquainted with the guys who live around here to find out if we can get them in our program. Do any of you guys use the Club?"

(We have found it most helpful for the worker to end his self-introduction with a question. This almost always effectively starts the conversation. The worker who makes an imperative self-presentation

["And I want you guys to be sure to come over and use the Club!"]
to the group may find himself "hanging" when it is finished.)

Even the most open and engaging worker encounters some obstacles in making initial contact with street-corner groups. He may
be met with a cold, hostile silence and Bogart-type stares. In this
case we found that a sense of humor is an indispensable ingredient
in breaking the ice. The worker continues, "What's wrong?" Again
he parries with a question. He opens them up. He makes opportunities for response.

The response, however, can be one of jeering and verbal abuse
such as, "Hey guys, look at this guy, he wants us to come join the
Boys' Club." "What are you, some kind of nut or something?" "We
wouldn't be caught dead in that place." "Get lost!"

We treated such negative responses as though they were motivated
by playful humor. We did not avoid what was said. Our workers
would respond with, "Why wouldn't you be caught dead in a Boys'
Club?" "Why do you want me to get lost?"

Another common thrust at the worker by the new group is, "Why
do you say you want to help us? What's in it for you, man?" One
of our workers said that he would answer that line of questioning by
replying first that he was a professional youth worker and that his
livelihood depended on his work with young people. Then he would
go on to say that he would much rather work with kids than with
adults because kids aren't so set in their ways. And he would remind
them that he grew up in a neighborhood like this and would have
appreciated having someone older to talk with and a program of
some kind in which to participate.

The same worker reports that on occasion a member of a group
would accuse him of misrepresenting himself as a youth worker;
that he was really a cop. The worker would capitalize on this accusa-
tion by inquiring, "What makes you think I'm a cop?" He reports
that a discussion of the police frequently would follow and would
reveal important information about the new group's attitudes toward
law enforcement and authority in the community.

There also are occasions when a worker will encounter overt
threats from a group he is trying to make contact with for the first
time. He will be greeted with, "Get the hell out of here or we'll beat

the hell out of you!" At that point the worker might say, "Seems like I came at the wrong time. I'm going now, but I'll be back [tell them precisely *when* you will be back] to talk to you again about the whole thing."

Some of our workers chose to make contact with a new group by concentrating on certain members. They found that by establishing contact with perhaps only one member they could later obtain a casual, easy introduction to the entire group. Developing friendships with ex-members of groups who are older but who return to the haunts of the old club can prove to be a valuable entree for contacting street groups.

The worker who has mobility is also in a position to make contacts more quickly and easily. Our worker would pull up in a Boys' Club station wagon to a street group on a corner (he knew in advance that they liked sports) and say, "You guys play basketball? I'm lookin' for some guys to take on the Rangers down at the Park District courts."

The styles and methods of contacting street groups are as varied and as complex as the personalities, resources and knowledge of the workers. But we found that the highly publicized, stereotyped technique of workers "hanging around" a lunch counter or a pool hall for several days or weeks in order to "get close" to a group is unnecessary. We concluded that the use of the indirect approach to young people is a waste of valuable time and money and indicates a serious misconception about the human needs and responses of youngsters on the street.

We found that the most common experience at the initial approach to a group is that street groups are interested in what you have to offer and conversation proceeds freely and normally. You just move in and start talking.

The Major Program Settings
for Out-Reach Work:
Outposts and Autos

CASUAL observers of youngsters in deprived neighbor-hoods, and especially of street groups, frequently characterize them as being "hard-to-reach" and "alienated." This is a superficial judg-ment and tends to imply that such youngsters do not share the behavior and attitudes of middle-class or more advantaged young people. The research conducted on our project by the Institute for Social Research of the University of Michigan tended to indicate that this was more true of behavior than of attitudes or values. Actually, from an *attitudinal* point of view, street-group members are "joiners" who want to participate in group activities. Far from being hard-to-reach or alienated, such youngsters, when approached through the direct contact methods of good out-reach work, exhibit the same middle-class propensity for joining as the Elks or Kiwanis; but they want to join and be part of a social organization on their own terms.

In the early stages of our project we thought we could "pick up" street groups on the neighborhood corners and simply "feed" them into a boys club or other conventional youth-serving agency. While this is not impossible to do, it is not easy because the building-based youth-serving agency has some "alienating" qualities about it. For one thing, the conventional youth-serving agency tends to serve younger age groups than the age group that constitutes the core of the gang problem. Any youth-serving agency with a relatively large age range for membership, let us say eight to eighteen, will tend to accumulate and hold more of its younger members because their mothers encourage them to go there, or actually bring them there for supervised play activities. From the mother's point of view the boys club is a large-scale baby-sitting service for the eight- to thirteen-year-olds, and from the boys club's point of view it becomes necessary to devise much of their program to suit this age range. From the older teenager's point of view, however, the boys club or youth-serving agency is defined by the predominant age group to be found there. As such, the conventional youth-serving agency comes to be defined as "a place where little kids go," and this definition has serious consequences when efforts are made to attract older boys.

At the same time, if a youth-serving agency is, indeed, largely inhabited by younger children, then it becomes important to the staff to protect the younger members from the stronger and more sophisticated boys who might enter the same building. It is considerations of this kind, combined with the desire of the staff to provide younger children with models of good behavior, that give rise to a multitude of rules about conduct that are seen as unnecessary restrictions by older teenagers who are eager to grow up and be their own masters. As such, rules about removing hats, rough language, smoking and roughhousing that are designed to protect the younger boy also serve to "alienate" the older boy, and especially the street-group member. In process of time all these characteristics of the conventional youth-serving agency combine into an organized system and become institutionalized. The younger population's availability gives rise to programming for them and this, in turn, means that economic investment is made in such programming, and it becomes progressively more difficult and more expensive to change the organization, program and rules to accommodate the older teenager or the street-group member.

In this context it becomes an open question as to who is alienated from whom. Is the street-group boy alienated from the conventional youth-serving agency or has the latter with its younger population, children's program and protective rules alienated the gang boy? Certainly, it depends on whom the youth-serving agency wants to serve and what it wants to do. If the youth-serving agency wants to reach the gang boy and change his behavior and attitudes, it must come to grips with the problem of attracting such clients and maintaining relations with them long enough to be an influence in their lives. First of all this means devising some strategy that will *appear* to lower the standards of ideal middle-class morality. But it is only a strategy, and this must be clearly understood.

If the conventional youth-serving agency with its relatively formal atmosphere of programs and rules is perceived as a negativistic environment by the gang member, then an interim strategy of expanding the tolerance limits of the agency must be decided upon. Similarly, if street-group boys prefer their own style of freedom and adventure and will only relate to a youth-serving agency that can successfully compete with, or supply, the degree of freedom and adventure that will attract and hold them, then the agency that is desirous of reaching and influencing them must find some way of providing such services as an operating strategy. This does not mean that the agency or its staff must tolerate illegal behavior or foster other undesirable traits. What it does mean is that the agency must have its goals clearly in view and must go about its work in such a way as to give itself a chance to implement them. Accordingly, a way must be found to tolerate behavior *in the early stages of a relationship that will not be tolerated later,* and to use the intervening time to influence the street-group member in a conforming direction. Clearly, what is needed is something in the nature of a decompression chamber where a series of cathartic experiences can be had before new pressures are applied. Similarly, an atmosphere of freedom, adventure and some degree of privacy, that is, associating with one's own age group, must be created if the street-group boy is to be reached successfully.

Some of the characteristics of a desirable setting for street work are implicit in the analysis that has been made above. In the absence of the ability to create such a setting some youth-serving agencies take the easy way out and simply join the gang boy on the street. This method of procedure throws the entire burden of influencing the street group on the personal qualities and charisma of the outreach worker and it forces him to compete directly with the distractions of street life. While this is a necessary procedure for contacting the street group, it is far from ideal as a setting for maintaining the intensity and stability of a relationship that is intended to serve as a vehicle for transmitting influence from a worker to the gang, or to its separate members. There may well be occasions when a relationship on the street is the only one that can be established or maintained, but if it can be brought into a setting with a higher potential for influence, then that change ought to be made.

In the CYDP we came to rely upon two program settings that tended to satisfy the requirements of working with street groups. They had degrees of tolerance, freedom and adventure for the older teenager that the conventional youth-serving agency ordinarily lacks, and they had the added advantages of helping to create the illusion of privacy, ownership and diversity of program. The first of these was The Outpost and the second was The Auto (actually station wagons). Let us consider these, one after the other, setting forth their major characteristics and the rationale for using them in the ways we did.

The Outpost

An outpost can be any building, or a part of a building like a storefront, a basement or even an apartment. It is important that it have easy accessibility from the street and that it either have, or can be made to have, some internal diversity so that it can accommodate more than one activity at a time. Of primary importance is the fact that, if it is avoidable, it should *not* have some prior definition as a public or private agency (e.g., it should not simply be a room *in* a school, church, police station or conventional youth-serving agency), for that definition will tend to color the preconceptions, perceptions and future operations of The Outpost. The idea is to free the place from the traditions and prejudices of both the existing youth-serving agencies and the future client population.

In the case of the CYDP, we rented an old fire-insurance-patrol building which, for all practical purposes, resembled a regular fire station. It was a two-story building measuring perhaps 40 by 120 feet. It was located on a side street but within two blocks of a large high school, an upper-grade center (sixth, seventh and eighth grades) and a grammar school. It was also within three blocks of a park which consisted mainly of three baseball diamonds, and was two-thirds of a mile distant from the boys club that served as the administrative base of the CYDP project staff in that area. All of these were important auxiliaries for either reaching the youth population, working with them or gaining services for them. All of this is to say that an outpost location must take such factors into account.

The first floor of the fire house consisted of two large rooms, one behind the other. The first room, where the fire engines used to park, was converted into a large assembly room which could be used to hold dances and social or larger group meetings. The second room, where the fire engines used to be serviced, was fitted with a workbench and drains in the floor. This became an ideal place for boys to wash cars and venetian blinds to make some money and to tinker with cars and learn elementary automechanics. We bricked up the sally-port at the front of the building and placed an office at the front to enable us to control the youth population entering and leaving the building.

The second floor of the fire house consisted of three large rooms, one behind the other. There was a front office, a large dormitory where the firemen used to sleep and a rear lounge where they spent their free time. The office we left alone, the dormitory we partitioned off into three small meeting rooms and the lounge we used as was. In many ways this was an ideal building for an outpost and it took a minimum of effort to make it functional, but the point is that any building selected for an outpost must have the capacity to become functional in some of the ways outlined above.

There is a great temptation to transform an outpost into a smaller version of a conventional youth-serving agency and *this temptation must be resisted*. An outpost is a program setting and one of the main elements in the CYDP out-reach program was informal counseling. Accordingly, an outpost must be furnished in such a manner as to promote informal counseling relations and opportunities between the workers and the youth. For practical purposes this means that an outpost should be minimally furnished. It should have chairs, tables, sofas and desks, but very little of the usual youth-serving agency paraphernalia, e.g., ping-pong tables, games, etc. The reasons for this should be clear. The purpose of an outpost is to promote talk, discussion, counseling. When youngsters are engaged in the traditional youth-serving agency games (ping-pong, pool, checkers, cards) they are relating only to *each other* and the objects that comprise the physical equipment of the games. One of the major tasks that confront the worker is to serve as a counter-influence to negative peer-group influences. It is, therefore, important that the physical setting and equipment of the outpost serve to encourage association and discussion *between the staff and their clients.* Games and physical objects tend to isolate youngsters from the staff and make it convenient for the staff to avoid personal involvement with youth while, at the same time, giving the appearance that everyone is "busy and involved." But the fact of the matter is they are not. Actually, while youngsters are involved in traditional games, the staff is excluded and reduced to a relatively passive role. The predominant character of youth activity under such circumstances is that the peer group continues to socialize itself and, if the nature of that socialization process contains negative influences, these will continue to be communicated. On the other hand, if the outpost is relatively "stripped" of the usual games-room equipment, this convenient escape route from social interaction is closed and the staff and their clients are "forced" into association and cross-talk. That, after all, is the main object of the outpost and talk is the medium of social influence between out-reach workers and youth.

It is, of course, necessary to have some equipment for the socials and dances that may be held in an outpost from time to time. Thus, if live music is not available, a good record player will be needed. Older teenagers like music in any case and recorded music, if properly selected, can serve as the basis for many a discussion that can lead to other topics. Similarly, it it advisable to have a TV set available, but its use should be in full control of the staff so that TV programs can serve as a point of departure for bull sessions and counseling. A large bulletin board will also serve many useful functions for both the youth and the staff. One thing we did with the CYDP Outpost, which may be considered unusual, is that we hung many good works of modern art (reproductions) by famous painters on the walls. Many of these provoked discussion, (e.g., "What's that supposed to be?"), and were a stimulus to further explorations in the world of art, literature, poetry and music.

We did not *publicly* define the Outpost as a place where "problem boys" were dealt with, nor did we make overt reference to the underlying task of preventing and controlling juvenile delinquency;

that is why our project was called the Chicago *Youth Development* Project, *not* the Chicago Anti-delinquency Project. It is difficult enough to deal with the problems of youngsters in deprived areas without contributing to them by reinforcing a negative self-image of youngsters whose self-concept you are trying to change in positive ways. We went to considerable lengths avoiding that kind of identification of ourselves and our clients, including the avoidance of publicity in the mass media or fund-raising public-relations gestures and we believe we succeeded in evading such negative, stereotyping imagery.

The atmosphere of the Outpost was kept informal and relaxed. It was perceived by the youngsters as a comfortable place to visit and few unnecessary or bureaucratic demands were placed on them— especially at first. There was very little that the youngster felt he *had* to do, but conditions had been so arranged that by doing what could readily be done, *i.e.*, meeting the staff and talking, the youth did what it was that we wanted them to do. A visitor to the Outpost might find many different kinds of activities going on all over the place: (a) highly-structured counseling between one worker and two boys being conducted in the upstairs office; (b) a well-run club meeting going on in one of the three upstairs meeting rooms with a worker looking in on it occasionally; (c) three or four youngsters having a running and shouting exchange of greetings and quick information as they pass each other on the stairs; (d) a girls' group meeting in the downstairs social room, planning the decorations for Friday night's social; (e) a supervisor using the phone in the downstairs office trying to arrange for a bus for an outing on Saturday; and (f) an out-reach worker "hanging" with some youngsters just in front of the Outpost and having an eye on the traffic going in and out the door; etc. We wanted interaction between the staff and the clients and in this fluid situation we got it. Interestingly enough, we seldom heard a youth complain, "There ain't nothing to do at the Outpost."

All of this social interaction added up to a unique kind of group work. In ordinary group-work practice a group using democratic group processes meets to plan and discuss their own programs with the help of a group worker. At the Outpost groups met to discuss everything and anything with their workers. Most group club meetings had no agenda and no apparent or predetermined goals. The meeting itself was its own end as far as the youngsters were concerned. From the staff point of view, however, not only was group process an end in itself, it was also a means toward an end, *i.e.*, it was being used as a vehicle for socialization, the rehearsal of roles, and the allocation of expectations and responsibilities. It was one of the main arenas for playing the reciprocity game ("I will do this, if you will do that; Joe will do this, if Jim will do that."). We saw group process as the means for attempting to achieve all this and the Outpost was one of the major settings where it could be pursued with relatively little distraction.

The Outpost was ordinarily kept open from 2:00 P.M. to 10:00 P.M. and, especially in the early stages of the project, any young man or woman could wander in off the street and take part in the activities and discussions going on there. Frequently, the youngsters our workers brought in from the streets would, in turn, bring in still others on their own so that, in process of time, straight on-the-street out-reach work became less necessary. Nevertheless, our workers were encouraged to spend at least one day a week on the streets, despite a full case load of seventy-five to one hundred group members, so that they would not be the "victims" of self-selected communication networks that might produce a false, partial or distorted picture of what was going on in the streets of the neighborhood. Eventually, even the CYDP staff was forced to resort to some bureaucratic procedure, *i.e.*, we issued Outpost membership cards to the eighteen to twenty-five groups who regularly used the Outpost; but these identification cards were mainly used to give priority to the regulars when socials, dances or other special events took place at the Outpost.

The Outpost staff paid more attention to actual behavior than to symbolic behavior, and was more interested in preventing the more serious violative behavior than the less serious; it was all a question of balancing timing, priorities, conformity standards and the maintenance of relationships in order to exert influence. In this scheme of things, taking off hats, smoking, swearing and wearing rough-looking clothes (symbolic behavior) were less important than honoring one's promises or performing up to expectations. Similarly, individual fighting was less serious than group fighting; drinking was less serious than taking drugs; or truancy was less serious than stealing; even though all aspects of such behavior would ultimately come under review in appropriate cases as the workers interacted with the boys. As such, we did not require that boys remove their hats during visits to the Outpost, nor did we have a ban against smoking. Running and shouting in the Outpost was not discouraged unless and until it badly interfered with some other ongoing activity. After all, there was very little that could be spoiled or damaged and the youngsters tended to help control each other most of the time. If a youngster came into the Outpost with liquor on his breath, or even drunk, he was not pushed back out on the streets. Not only would the workers talk to him, and protect him from the immediate consequences of his foolishness by seeing to it that he was delivered at home responsibly that night, but they would eventually try to deal with the causes of the drinking problem itself. The youths who came to the Outpost soon began to realize that the CYDP staff was not spending a great deal of time shouting about the traditional youth-serving agency rules to them. The pressures for conformity were more subtle and insidious, and reached behind the obvious, surface manifestations that so preoccupy the the unsophisticated. As a consequence, many of the social clubs among the youth who attended the Outpost began to formulate their own rules about surface behavior because they felt they could deal with it. Some of these rules were far stricter than any that a youth agency might impose, e.g., fines for swearing, or being kicked out of the group if three meetings were missed. Fortunately, the young do not differ much from the old in this respect for both make up more rules than they are willing to seriously enforce. Nevertheless, despite the disparity between rule-making and sporadic short-term enforcement, such activities gave the young people some valuable experiences in the nature of social processes and the minimum requirements for getting along together. More important, however, was the whole range of talk and activities between boys and staff designed to enable them to cooperate in their own socialization through the guidance of out-reach workers who knew what they were doing.

The Station Wagon

To most people an automobile is simply a convenient mode of transportation and, on the symbolic level, it may serve as a status pretension; but for the CYDP staff the station wagons of the project were a major program setting, that is, they were conceived as and functioned as "mobile counseling chambers." It was a setting in which a worker and a gang boy or a group could interact either on the basis of a topic that arose out of personal matters or as a reaction to some phase of the passing scene that the worker or one of the boys fixed upon as a point of departure to stimulate further discussion. If the reader will think about it he will see many analogies between a station wagon loaded with a worker and a group of youngsters and a meeting room in the Outpost. In both situations the worker has what amounts to a "captive audience" and discussion takes place either out of spontaneous interaction or an induced stimulus guided by the worker. The main thing about this mobile counseling chamber (as is also true of the Outpost) is that the worker not allow himself or his clients to simply be the passive "victims" of passing experience; that is, the worker must always be on the alert for the opportunities presented to him by the situation and play his counseling role to the maximum, It is, of course, both easier and more pleasant for the worker to pass the time of day in idle gossip and simple reaction to the prominent features of the passing scene, but you do not hire or train skilled out-reach workers so that they are merely entertained by their life experiences. In order to gain the maximum benefits from the potential inherent in this mobile counseling chamber the worker has to be self-aware and task-oriented in order to turn the experiences he and his clients are undergoing to good account.

In the early stages of the project, or in the early stages of a relationship with a newly contacted street group, the station wagon had a seductive function, that is, in order to introduce street-group members to the Outpost, our workers had to go out into the streets and bring them in. The station wagon with its promise of mobility served as an inducement for youngsters to enter into the minimal relationship with the worker in order to "go for a ride"; to see and to be seen, to feel that something was happening and that the pace of life and experience had quickened. Although this kind of an inducement might be offered by any kind of a car that was capable of locomotion, we found that the strength of the inducement increased in direct proportion to the newness and good appearance of the vehicle. Had the mere initial contacting of boys been our only objective, we would have been a howling success with a fleet of Lincoln Continentals, Cadillacs and Chrysler Imperials; but the car had to have some functional features as well. What was needed was a vehicle that had a special appeal in itself—snob appeal, if you please. It had to be "sharp" and large enough to haul a large number of youngsters around the city.

We chose large-model station wagons and the only extra equipment we put in them was a radio. No identifying marks of any kind were placed on them because, like the Outpost, we wanted our vehicles to have not only high prestige but also an air of informality. We always used the trip-ticket method for control purposes, but the out-reach workers always had the freedom to just "cruise" the area, especially in those early days of the project. We considered that the vehicle was being put to good use whenever a worker and youngsters were in it. The worker did not have to have a destination. We saw the vehicle as a "mobile counseling chamber," a setting in which interaction between a worker and a young man or group could take place. (For examples of the kind of counseling and interaction that boys and workers experienced in the station wagon see the chapter, "Informal Counseling Techniques for Individuals and Groups.")

Erik H. Erickson in his book, *Childhood & Society*, spoke of the restless mobility which characterizes adolescents. During adolescence the human musculature is growing into its full development. A young man literally does not know his own strength. He is testing and exploring it constantly. His body, and by extension, his whole world are *terra incognita* and this restless, searching curiosity seems almost insatiable. We found that our style of using a vehicle tied in functionally with these adolescent developments. Our workers took advantage of the "stimulus hunger" of the gang boys and provided them with new sights, sounds and experiences which they could assimilate. The workers knew exactly what they were doing. They deliberately turned station-wagon rides into learning experiences. They did not permit the environment to float by passively. They helped the youth groups in the station wagon to approach and encounter the world they viewed from inside.

A conversation we had with one of our more experienced outreach workers near the end of the project serves to summarize the importance of both the Outpost and the station wagons as settings for out-reach work. We asked this worker what justification he thought there was to the establishment of an Outpost and he replied as follows:

"I would say in one word—talk. And by that I mean that you can sincerely and effectively counsel a boy because of the surroundings you have, the attitude that the boy has toward these surroundings and the attitude he has toward you.

"The Outpost is very unstructured in the sense that what goes on here depends on the people that are involved. We have the kind of talk programs that the staff and the youth we serve are honestly interested in. In fact, they help us plan it. This gives them a great feeling of participation. They feel that they belong here and that this building belongs to them.

"I'll give you an example. Today Robert and I went to the garage where we have our station wagons serviced. While we were there we looked over some new cars and Robert said, 'This new station wagon doesn't seem as long as our station wagon.' Now, he didn't say 'your' station wagon or 'the Boys Club' station wagon—he said 'our' station wagon. And in reality Robert actually feels that the station wagon, in part, belongs to him. And he feels this Outpost building, in part, is his."

Thus, we feel that it is this deep sense of participation and belonging which the Outpost and the use of the station wagons help foster. They provide our workers with a good atmosphere and setting for the "talk" programming used to bridge the gap between the gangs in the street and the youngsters in the traditional, but sometimes "alienating" youth-serving agency.

Making Positive Changes in
Status Relations Between
Street Gangs

THE social relations between the various street gangs in the areas where our project went forward seemed, in many ways, to resemble a microcosm of the contemporary international political order. Ordinarily, an uneasy balance of power was maintained among street gangs through the use of overt or implied threats, public posturing about how "tough" and ready for defense each group was, and a constant process of testing the limits of honor or territory which sometimes led to an outbreak of violence. Each street gang had only the most obvious and superficial knowledge about the other so there was a great deal of talk and name-writing on walls in a mutual effort of all to impress the others. Occasionally one gang would either commit a serious act, or get blamed for it, or take credit for it since the actual perpetrators were unknown, and then the event would be common gossip, or actually get into the newspapers. The gang whose name was linked to the event would make some effort to capitalize on their transient notoriety by bragging and inflating their tough reputation. A whole series of such events in the history of the area, some recent and some remote, and some hardly more than the myths and folklore of the streets, gave rise in process of time to a rough sorting of groups into a crude version of a barnyard pecking order. Those gangs which were presumed to be larger and tougher were considered to be on the top of the heap, and the smaller and weaker groups were on the bottom, with a rough-and-ready relative sorting of those in between. In ordinary circumstances it was a loose form of social order which even permitted the existence of unaffiliated cliques and individuals; but in times of crises, when the area was presumed to be in danger of imminent attack by outsiders, or when some gang or another felt its honor or its women had been insulted, the social order of the young would be transformed and the unaffiliated would hasten to make alliances, or at least verbally identify themselves, with one of the existing groups, for at times of crises "You're either with us or against us," and neutrals are suspect.

At the time that the CYDP staff first entered the two areas where the project was conducted, this process of social sorting had been going on for so long without any counter-forces to exert pressure in the direction of conformity that there were no known, established street groups whose reputation could be said to have been based on conforming behavior. In a bad situation, where each street gang had exerted itself to look and act tougher than the next, not unlike the international situation, the key to survival seemed to be a tough reputation as a deterrent to the aggression of others, who were also busy looking and acting tough to deter everyone else.

In such a seeming "dog-eat-dog" world, the youngsters who sought to avoid delinquency and had an interest in participating in conventional behavior were numerous but much less visible. Their "problem" was that they were unorganized and they were outside the recognized social order. The delinquent gangs were not attractive to them and, under ordinary circumstances, they were not attractive to the gang. The more conforming youngsters were considered "square" and no public recognition was awarded to their conventional conduct because the delinquent-tending value system of the gangs publicly identified as having a tough reputation set the local standards of how to come to public notice. The way to attract attention was to be bad, or at least to be considered bad, and thus monopolize the goods, services and status available which made up the "rep" and maintained the leadership in the pecking order.

One street gang we worked with in the early days was so self-conscious of its public image that it "went Madison Avenue" and appointed a club historian whose function it was to clip all news items appearing in the press about the gang. This was unusual but indicative. Most gangs simply relied upon, and contributed to, the rumor chains and gossip of the streets to communicate the quality of their "rep" to the neighborhood. In gang-infested areas many members of the community, both juvenile and adult, seemed to gain some vicarious satisfaction from repeating the events, folklore and myths of gang exploits, much of which when traced turned out to be simple attribution, imputation or other products of mutual recrimination that may or may not have had some kernel of truth in them. While such rumor and gossip networks are high on volume and speed, they are low on accuracy, but they serve the purposes of delinquent gangs quite well as a method of inflating their insecure egos. In addition, the distinctive and colorful style of clothing, complete with emblems or symbols, that was frequently worn by gang members, served to attract attention not only to themselves but to the fact that others did not "belong." Finally, the peculiar ambivalence toward knives and guns (the latter usually the property of older brothers, fathers or uncles), which were obviously concealed or meaningfully "flashed" (why have a concealed weapon if nobody knows it?), as if to objectify an inner insecurity, was evident frequently enough to help contribute to a "tough-bad" image and a local "rep."

Our workers, then, faced the task of providing individuals who were inclined to belong to conventional groups an opportunity to achieve a reputation through group experiences which would be meaningful within the context of the high delinquent values of the street.

The delinquent values of the street could not easily be dismissed. There is a certain romance, a fervor, a dash and excitement to gang activities on the street which makes much conventional behavior seem drab by comparison. We had to face the fact that while street fighting and crime may be dangerous, it also is viewed by the gangs as fun; a sort of sporting life. And so we had to initiate the establishment of a new hierarchy on the premise that *high visibility* and dramatic, intense personal involvement in group activities are the potent ingredients in achieving status in the street-group society. Any alternative to the delinquent style of street life, we felt, must be competitively spectacular and leave lasting, memorable consequences. Thus, we decided to have a ball, literally.

We decided that our group ought not simply to have socials like anyone else; they had to have "Big Dances," which meant formal and semi-formal dress, bands and entertainment, and a dance hall—not merely a gym or a church basement. We were able to help the groups obtain publicity, in the form of local radio and newspaper announcements and celebrity drop-in visits which added to the "something special" atmosphere. The dance simply had to be "fabulous" and above all, there could afford to be *no trouble* (see chapter, "Conducting a Successful Dance in a High-delinquency Area").

We found that groups who were able to hold such affairs became *known* as "the group which held that fabulous affair" and not as "that head-bustin', hum-bugging" group. So we helped first one and then another of our groups do some of the following things to make a "fabulous affair" a reality:

1. We hired a good, local dance band plus acts like singing and dancing groups. (We sometimes hired *two* dance bands when possible in order to keep the music going.)

2. The sponsoring club members all wore their best clothes or at least distinctive, conventional clothes. In a few cases, formal gowns and tuxedo suits were worn.

3. We hired a professional, uniformed, usher service to help in crowd-control measures.

4. The women guests were presented with corsages, and the men wore lapel flowers.

5. We held buffet suppers prior to the dance to help create a festive atmosphere.

6. We held the dances in commercial dance halls and controlled the guest list.

7. We arranged for celebrities from the sports and entertainment worlds to "drop in" and be introduced from the stage, or to simply make "an appearance."

At this point you may be wondering how, in lower-income areas of the city, we were able to finance this. It was a joint effort. Our workers were given allowances with which they could help finance, say, the deposit necessary for a dance hall. More often than not our workers were able to arrange for credit with the various commercial outlets that serviced the dance. Admission to the dance averaged $1.50 and the income from a highly successful evening sometimes resulted in a $300 to $400 profit for the sponsoring club.

The weeks of planning that went into these "fabulous affairs" helped introduce many of the youngsters we worked with to the problems of making decisions about how much food to order; which hall should be used for the dance; how much punch five-hundred people can drink in one evening; who will be responsible for decorating the tables; who will introduce the celebrities; who will handle the publicity, etc.

Our workers tried to provide a setting where the boys themselves could make these decisions (even if in some cases they were obviously making wrong decisions, such as not ordering enough food) so that they could learn from their mistakes and the democratic committee process. We found that this experience in committee bureaucracy, which preceded the "fabulous affair," had lasting effects on some of the boys as they later related themselves to school and work.

We were able to provide a number of other important, spectacular and highly visible conventional activities for the boys with whom we worked. When sharecroppers in Tennessee were driven off their farms in 1961 because of their voter-registration efforts, we organized groups to gather food for the trucks which were being sent from Chicago to the "Tent City" that had been established for the sharecroppers in Fayette County. Participation in this and other projects in the civil-rights movement gave a sense of dignity and pride to many of our groups—especially the Negro groups. Our workers took groups to the big civil-rights rallies in Chicago where the boys acted mainly as spectators; but word of their witness spread rapidly in the home neighborhoods and served as another antidote to the "rep" based on violence or toughness.

We also gave our groups an opportunity to make special trips to the opera and to downtown theaters.

It was our experience that groups which held such spectacular affairs became "known" for it, and over a period of time, and to some degree, the basis for awarding status in the local area tended to shift in a more conventional direction. Such groups, we found, were then willing to experiment with less spectacular conventional activities and even developed the skill and patience to do the necessary planning-committee work that must precede successful events. As a result the status relations between local youth groups changed so that the more conventional groups were accorded more status.

Confidentiality

AN out-reach worker inevitably comes to know about illegal acts committed by youths he knows. Very often there has been no arrest or apprehension. The police either do not know who did it or they haven't caught the guilty person yet. Should a worker report a youth to the police when he knows with some certainty that the youth is guilty of a crime?

Technically and legally the worker is required to report felonies to the police. Any person who has knowledge of a felony who does not report the felony can become an accessory which means, of course, that he is liable to prosecution himself.

However, certain people are exempt from this—doctors, confessors and lawyers, for example, but only in cases where they are in a professional relationship to the person who has committed the felony. This exemption has been established by legal precedent. In the case of out-reach work, of course, no such precedent has been established as yet.

In fact and in practice, however, the out-reach worker sometimes acts as though the precedent had been established. So far as we know, no one has ever attempted to prosecute a youth worker for failure to report the commission of a minor crime. It seems to be generally assumed that the same confidentiality which obtains between doctor and patient and lawyer and client, obtains between the worker and the youth with whom he is in contact. If this were not the case out-reach work would become almost impossible to carry on.

The worker must be a person who can be trusted. It is conceivable, however, that in some cases a worker must turn someone in. If this is done, it should be done openly, not secretly. If you are going to call the police do not hide it. If you secretly inform the police and it is discovered, the trust which makes your work possible will be destroyed. What youths tell you about themselves is "privileged communication" and you should never betray their confidence. At the same time you cannot just stand there if a crime is being committed before your very eyes, even if it is by someone you know very well. Try to stop it. If you can't, tell the persons who are committing the crime that you are going to call the police. This, of course, involves risk but if youths know they can commit crimes in your presence with impunity your effectiveness as a worker will be negated.

We have really brought up this issue to show how difficult it can be. There are probably no absolutely valid rules or procedures to follow. The worker is very often straddling the horns of a dilemma and, often, all he can do is "ride the beast." The out-reach worker, like the policeman on the street, *must exercise discretion* and good judgment.

Building an Information
Network

IN order to be effective in his work, an out-reach worker must not only come to know the youth of his community but he must come to know many people and they, in turn, must come to know him. Since communities exhibit great diversities in population, housing and local institutions, it is one of the worker's earliest tasks to make an assessment of the local situation in his community and to decide upon a strategy of intervention that is most suitable. Generally speaking, this means that he must make contact and develop a series of relations with local influentials, community leaders, social agencies, and the institutions significant to youth welfare. Typically, this means contacting parents, school personnel, the police, local businessmen, potential employers, probation officers, public and private agency people, clergymen and local politicians. In a relatively short time such local adults and agency people should be entered in the worker's address book or file system and he must reciprocate help and favors or the relationship he has established will deteriorate and break. The worker views these various people, who may be useful to him, as a form of community organization that results in the development of an information network.

A worker needs as much information as he can possibly obtain in order to facilitate the making of contacts with new groups in the streets. He needs an even greater fund of information if he is to be effective in his ongoing work with street gangs and clubs. What he needs to develop, in effect, is a massive information network.

The worker is or should be a leader in the community he serves. He is a decision maker and like all leaders he faces the responsibility of gathering and receiving accurate and sufficient information upon which to base his decisions. An out-reach worker cannot sit back and wait for the information to roll in. He must operate as a good reporter operates; he must deliberately build a whole network of informants who will confide in him and to whom he can be useful.

The typical inner-city slum or housing project communities in which youth workers do their work appear to superficial observers to be disorganized. One might think that these communities are so lacking in organization that even a good reporter could not develop a good set of informants. We found this notion to be a myth. The communities in which we worked were highly organized, but the organization was not readily visible to the untrained eye. For example, some of the organization of these communities was designed to achieve goals and purposes which society at large has deemed illegitimate—goals such as making money through prostitution and gambling. These organized criminal efforts normally require an enormous amount of organization which is almost entirely hidden.

But whether the form of organization is legitimate or illegitimate the worker will have to be in touch with key people in the local community if he is to be informed about the real forces at play which will have a bearing on the lives of the youth with whom he works. Our informants included such diverse sources as agency staff people, candy-store and hot-dog-stand managers, newspaper-stand men, housing-project personnel, youth officers, waitresses, pool-hall owners, schoolteachers, and kids in the street groups. Most of these people are strategically located in the neighborhood so that other people are frequently talking to them or in front of them.

The good worker has a responsibility to cultivate these people and to gain their confidence. This means that he must spend a considerable amount of time in the street not only talking with these people but also *listening* to them. And above all, the worker must be casual and informal. He must be willing to invest time and energy in small talk with his informants so that they can get to know him and trust him. The workers must be candid enough to let the informant know his personal life. It is not enough for a worker to walk up to a candy-store owner in a time of crisis (such as when the worker has learned of a possible gang fight in the area) and coldly begin questioning him and expect much information.

Once the worker has established a friendly, casual relationship with a number of informants he can be more explicit about his needs. He would be best advised to take advantage of a situation which his informant has accidentally initiated such as when Tony, the candy-store owner, complained to one of our workers one day that he was afraid that one of the gangs in the area was going to attack another gang that evening. Our worker took advantage of this opening and responded something like this:

"You know, Tony, I'm glad you know about that because you may be able to help me. As you know I'm a street-club worker in this neighbor-hood and it's my job to keep the guys around here out of trouble, if I can. You hear a lot of things about what's going on in the neighborhood that could help me keep kids out of trouble or help them once they're in it. I hope you'll tell me, like you have just now, when you hear something I should know. At the same time, if any information you give me is con-fidential, you can be sure I won't use it in such a way as to betray your trust in me and I'll let you know if what I tell you is confidential. I'm not a policeman. I'm interested in keeping kids out of trouble and I know you are too. So I'd appreciate any help you can give me and in return I'll be sure to keep you posted on what I know about what's happening in the area."

While the worker should always be as casual as possible in his relationship with his informants he should be careful to develop a book of telephone numbers, addresses and other pertinent informa-tion about his sources. He, like a good reporter, should be careful to keep the identity of his sources confidential when information he receives from them is communicated in a confidential manner or is to be used in official proceedings or in dealings with others who may react in an unfavorable way. But he should try to see to it that he introduces fellow workers or supervisors to his informants as soon as possible so that more than one worker knows his "beat." At the same time, in listening to the information given out by a variety of informants, the sophisticated worker will do his best to evaluate the information and to guard himself against the possibility of being "used" to promote some inimical purpose. The communications net-work should be firmly established so that if a worker becomes ill or goes on vacation others will have an opportunity to use his resources.

The out-reach worker should visit his informants often and be careful not to be "strictly business." These people are not mere functionaries, but confidantes and colleagues. They are your eyes and ears and they can be your voice, too. If you want certain information to get around the neighborhood a good set of informants can be transformed from an information network into a broadcasting network.

Calling Upon Obligations or
"What Have You Done for Me Lately?"

WE have seen now how gangs and individuals can be contacted by the out-reach worker and how the worker can keep up on what is happening in the area. But you may wonder how a worker, frequently a stranger to the area where he works, can develop a significant relationship with the potentially or actively delinquent local youth. Why should kids in high delinquency areas bother to relate at all to a worker who seems to come out of nowhere to become involved in his life? What's the connection or is it just a matter of superficial *contact?*

The ingredient which makes this relationship possible is the one which makes so many social relationships a reality—the element of reciprocity. It is the old business of giving in order to get; to exchange. You do something for me; I do something for you.

Reciprocity is the lubricant for a social system comprised of many sets of opposing pairs in which the separate halves of the pairs are dependent upon each other for fulfillment. Male and female, predator and prey, leader and follower, individual and group, man and society. "Self" does not exist without the "other." Doctors need patients, wage earners need employers, etc. We live in a social system of mutually interacting, mutually dependent individuals.

Now let's take a look at how this system of reciprocity works with street clubs or gangs. In the early stages of relating to individual kids or groups, we found that the workers did most of the giving. We had resources for which the kids hungered. We could offer rides in a station wagon, small loans, a place to meet, sports, socials, status through being in association with us and many other goods or services. But what keeps this process of the worker giving

53

and the youth getting from just going on and on? When does the worker start getting and why?

A new out-reach worker is in serious error if he thinks the youth he will be working with are completely amoral, antisocial, and totally alienated hoods. We found that most young people were normally intensely loyal to an ethical notion that boiled down to "You do something for me and I'll do something for you." They felt that if you did something for someone he was *obligated* to you. They felt that you had the *right* to ask for something in return and that it was the *duty* of the other, if at all possible, to give it to you.

And so, once our worker had laid up a series of obligations with a group he was able to begin calling them in. He could make it known that he expected to see Johnny in school on time, or that Tony would stop staying out all night, or that George would lay off the bottle. The worker's success in doing this depended, of course, on the appropriateness and relevance of his requests.

It is a tricky process. Sometimes groups would take the attitude of "Yeah, but what have you done for us lately?" And so a worker plays it cool. He learns that it is best never to show all his cards at once; that is, he learns to avoid saying "after *all* I've done for you!" except as a last resort, but lets his record of accomplishments speak for itself. We found that if a worker was meaningful and relevant to the group's needs, they usually knew it and reciprocated. When our worker failed to develop real relationships with groups, no amount of talk on his part changed it. Deeds counted, not words.

There are, of course, persons who are so far "out of it" that they will not participate in this basic human reciprocity pattern. Sometimes this will be a leader of a gang who rules through force and coercion, and influences in a negative way, the lives of those kids who follow him. (There are, to be sure, many gangs led by "idea" men, not bullies.)

This negative influencer may or may not be seen by his group as a leader. But when it is clearly the case that a particular member of a group manages either to keep his group from involvement in constructive activities or involves them in delinquency by his influence the worker is faced with the responsibility of subverting and undermining this leader's influence.

This leader usually is a tough boy whose leadership is clearly based on physical prowess. He is a natural conservative and he is the one to whom the other members of the group defer. He enforces his will by the exercise of his veto power. The veto power is backed up by physical force, if necessary.

The worker encounters this veto power when he suggests a constructive activity for the group. The leader steps in and kills the activity by labeling it as "too square." Thus he establishes what we have come to refer to as "leadership in a do-nothing situation."

The worker soon learns it is difficult if not impossible to use this leader's veto power for constructive purposes. Do-nothing leaders have developed a reputation for omnicompetence, but they try to prevent the testing of this myth by vetoing test situations which would enable other members of the gang to judge them. Going here or there, or doing this or that are beneath the dignity of this negative influencer. It's "kid stuff," "too square" or "not cool." Under these circumstances, the group as a whole tends to spend its time just "hanging around" in a restricted area. Their conversation and interaction is limited to the narrow sphere of personal experiences and surface phenomena of the local scene. Their situation can be summed up in the frequently heard conversational gambit: "What's happening, man?" "Nothin', man."

Since the worker's interaction with the group is effectively checkmated by the veto power of a leader who maintains a do-nothing situation, the worker changes tactics. Perhaps he may even be taken in by the leader's bragging about how good he is, and all the things he can do. In any case, the worker decides to cultivate the leader in order to make him a better leader. The worker's notion at this point of decision seems to be that, if he can reform the dictator, the benefit to the group will be a benign despotism rather than sheer tyranny and that this will constitute a more promising atmosphere in which to do constructive work. Thus the worker begins by exposing the leader, alone, to new experiences. He offers the leader a more privileged association, he shares more information with him and extends him resources that he does not offer the others. If the do-nothing leader can be brought to respond to these overtures, no matter from what motives, a fateful process is set in train. He is caught in a network of human reciprocity relations and is slowly maneuvered into a do-something situation.

It may be that, at the outset, the do-nothing leader, is "going along with the program" out of the most cynical of motives, simply, to exploit the worker in all possible ways. To play this game, however, there has to be maintained a minimum relationship, to give the appearance of cooperation, to mislead the worker and to keep him "on the string." In this stage of the relationship the do-nothing leader who is acting out of cynical motives pretends to respond positively to the preachments of the worker, and he gives voice to the sentiments the worker would like to hear him express. There are promises not to get whiskey for the group next Saturday night, or vague and far-fetched plans about returning to school someday, or a half-expressed interest in vocational training or a job, none of which he entertains very seriously. If he is a good actor he creates a sufficient impression upon the worker to make him act upon these phony sentiments by actively seeking the resources and procedures to respond to these falsely expressed needs. In other cases the worker is fully aware of the game that is being played but he hopes against hope that he can successfully entrap the do-nothing leader despite these elaborate charades. On the other hand, there are some do-nothing leaders who respond to the worker's cultivation processes out of genuine motives. They view their special relationship to the worker as further recognition of their leadership capacity and, although they still maintain tight control over the status quo in their group, they tend to be more accepting of the opportunities that the worker offers to them on a personal basis. Such do-nothing leaders sometimes assume the role of "assistant" to the worker, or the worker informally confers this status on them.

It is our observation that, in the majority of such cases, as soon as the do-nothing leader is maneuvered into a do-something situation a process of status degradation sets in, for he almost invariably fails. If the worker gets him a job, he quits or gets himself fired. If the school authorities have been persuaded to take him back, he is soon cutting classes and gets expelled. If he is taken to a vocational school, he does not seem to have the motivation to pass the entrance tests. Although he may be a good street fighter, he is less good at sports and frequently refuses to participate. Such failures may more frequently reflect low motivation and disinterest in these kinds of pursuits than the absence of ability. Some do-nothing leaders display considerable ingenuity in pursuing their own concerns. In short, they may as often be unwilling as unable to perform. Nevertheless, as such experiences accumulate, the other members of the group begin to realize that their monolithic leader is a person who has failure experiences, and his supporting myth of omnicompetence begins to come apart at the seams. Although he does what he can to save face, neither his physical prowess nor his vehement denials about the significance of these failures can fully prevent the members of his group from having knowledge of what happened when his competence was brought to a test. In this respect, his veto power has effectively been neutralized.

A striking example of a do-nothing leader who was subverted through the sincere efforts of an out-reach worker is a boy whom we will call "B-jay." B-jay was the leader of a group called the "Reberls," who could always be found on "their corner." When the worker first tried to contact them, they remained suspicious and aloof. Persistent "hanging around" by the worker produced the comment from B-jay that the worker was probably "a fruit." The worker was not intimidated, but continued to come around and offer suggestions. B-jay told him to "get lost." Approaches to other members of the Reberls simply affirmed that B-jay was their spokesman. For several weeks B-jay parried the worker's efforts with remarks like, "The Reberls don't go swimming. This ain't no ball club. The Reberls wouldn't be found dead in the Boys Club." Nevertheless, B-jay accepted rides in the worker's station wagon. During the next few weeks, and after numerous car rides, it seemed to the worker that B-jay might be serious about his expressed desire "to have a job and get some money." The worker got him a job in a hotel, but in three days he quit. He said the boss was "riding" him. A few days later B-jay was arrested for street fighting, but the worker's intervention at the police station helped to convert the case into a station adjustment. In the next few weeks two more job experiences ended in failure. The next job was out of town, at a summer camp. After ten days B-jay was sent home because he "wouldn't work." The worker used these employment intervals to take the other Reberls on some trips through the city. When B-jay returned he vetoed these trips. A few days later he was arrested for strong-armed robbery and spent two weeks in custody. The worker went to court with him and he received six months' probation. Again the worker got him a job and this one he lost through being late and then absent. In disgust, B-jay decided to join the Army, but when the worker took him to the recruiting station, he did not pass the test.

Between B-jay's absences, at work or in custody, which the worker used to establish better relations with the group, and his failures, his leadership position began to be undermined. Some of the Reberls asked, "Where's all that money you were going to make and spend on us?" Or again, he would be asked, "When are you going to buy your own car?" Under such pressures, B-jay stopped vetoing the car rides offered to the Reberls by the worker. The worker used the car rides to propose an intra-group ball game at an early date. During the game it was established that B-jay was not a "star," in fact, on several occasions he was "butter-fingers." The worker next persuaded B-jay and the group to come into an outpost to plan a social. During that meeting, the worker actively solicited the participation of all the Reberls present and they responded. A week later, at the social, B-jay and several others arrived with liquor on their breath, and B-jay tried to smuggle the bottle in. The worker confiscated the bottle on the grounds that drinking "would just cause trouble and break up the social," and he was supported by the sober members of the Reberls. B-jay left the affair in drunken anger and several of the remaining Reberls expressed the sentiment that this was "all for the best." Over the next few months several cycles of events of the type described took place. B-jay was not "kicked out" of the Reberls, but was reprimanded by some of the members who would not have raised objections six months earlier. He was degraded in status, but did not fall to the bottom. The Reberls began to operate as a group with shared leadership, and the tenor of their behavior improved over what it had been. The more and less delinquent members of the group became visible cliques inside the Reberls.

What we have seen here is the history of a particular leader who worked from an extremely narrow base of physical prowess and delinquent behavior. He was provincial in every sense of the word, geographic, experiential and attitudinal. When attempts were made to broaden his base, by helping him to get employment and to lead his group in organized athletics or social events, he failed. Others in the group who had more capacity were enabled to emerge as leaders in their own right after the do-nothing leader had been debased in do-something situations. This made the group more accessible to the worker's influence and laid the groundwork for a higher potential of success in the future.

What Can an Out-Reach
Worker Do to Control
Gang Fighting?

DURING the six years that our project was in operation CYDP staff members were involved in attempts to control more than three hundred "gang fights" at all stages of their development: mainly imaginary, rumored, potential, or threatening, and a few that were real. In the light of this history we feel we have some basis for making some generalizations that may be helpful to others who find themselves in gang-conflict prevention.

Gang fights can have clear or obscure origins. They can arise from noble or base motives. They can result from real or imaginary precipitating incidents. They can start with the grievances of a single individual or with a group's conception of their needs for defense and offense. Notions of territory, status, sexual competition, freedom of mobility and the right to be left alone, all play a prominent role in gang fights but, because these notions are differentially defined by different individuals and groups, they are a source of dissension.

Gang fights can involve as few as three boys: two members of one group who "jump" a member of another group. The latter then goes to get his allies and the process can begin. Strictly speaking, this is a typical precipitating incident which is usually based on an alleged or real previous incident and so on, backwards, *ad infinitum*. For us, perhaps the most common situation has been the one in which a group of five to ten youngsters fight a similar-sized group. The largest gang fight we ever experienced involved thirty-five to forty boys battling another group of about the same size. But in six years of working in two of Chicago's "worst neighborhoods" on the West Side, this was the only actual gang fight on this scale that came to our attention.

Gang fights can take place at almost any time of the day or of the year but our experiences indicate the following probability factors in decreasing order of frequency: (1) On a hot, summer weekend evening. (2) On a hot, summer weekday evening. (3) In the late afternoon after the school day is over. (4) On a mild fall or spring evening during the school year. In short, they are times when youngsters are idle and thrown together out of doors; the temperature conditions may or may not serve as an aggravant.

Gang fights can take place almost anywhere. It is largely a question of the situation and the opportunity coming together. The fighting may take place along the street, on the corner, in the alleys, on vacant lots, school yards, public-housing grounds, hot-dog stands, drive-ins, and even inside modes of transportation like buses. Again it seems to be a case of youngsters either seeking each other out or being thrown together in a certain density that makes the place an "appropriate" one for a fight.

Gang fighting frequently involves the use of weapons. A bare-knuckles confrontation is not common. It is more characteristic of an individual fight. The weapons will include sticks, clubs, knives, chains, bricks (and anything else loose that can be thrown, such as pop bottles) and sometimes guns. Such guns as are used are frequently the property of older brothers, fathers, uncles, etc., and, more frequently than not, they are defective so that they are as great a danger to the user as to his "target."

The fighting groups usually know each other. We found that groups in conflict frequently have ambiguous feelings about each other. One of the most serious gang fights we experienced occurred the day after the groups had shared an enjoyable time together the previous evening. Gang fights can erupt for many reasons; some real and some imagined. A well-circulated rumor is potent enough to start trouble. One of the most common causes of group fighting is conflict over territory. Groups try to define what their "territory" is and invasion of those boundaries or conflict over whether or not one group's territory respects the needs of another group's mobility go to the core of many fights. (The scrawl of gang names and slogans on fences and walls is frequently an indication of the group's attempts to affirm its identity or territorial interest.)

Keeping in mind these general factors, we will summarize some important assumptions about gang fights which we found to be a sufficient ground for intervention.

In the majority of cases it is safe to assume that there are forces working in the direction of making the fight come off and there are forces working against the fight developing. We will describe these factions as Fight and No-Fight forces.

The natural human desire to avoid personal bodily injury is one of the main motivations of the No-Fight force. This faction of the gang has the same motivation you have. It is your responsibility to make these No-Fight forces stronger. Concentrate on developing, in a positive way, the ability of the No-Fight forces to express their view of the situation. It should be your strategy to have meetings with the opposing factions within a group in which you talk almost exclusively about the wisdom of the No-Fight choice. Do not provide a platform for the Fight faction to broadcast its point of view. It has been our experience that the "doves" listen to the "hawks" but that the hawks do not listen to the doves, so it is necessary to structure situations in which the voice of the hawks is muted. You may feel that this one-sidedness is undemocratic; but democracy works only when all factions agree on the rules and abide by the achieved consensus. The hawk forces of a gang bent on fighting frequently have not arrived at the level of citizenship at which consensus accommodation is attractive.

You can assume that *there will be no fight if everyone is permitted to save face.* This point cannot be emphasized too strongly. If you do not permit the Fight faction to save face they will fight. They may, in fact, fight you. The hawks should be allowed to maintain the impression that they would have fought "but." It is your job to provide the hawks with a "but."

A wide variety of face-saving possibilities exist and we will discuss some of them in our description of gang-fight control tactics in three general phases, initial, intermediate, and final.

During the *initial phase* there are numerous and fantastically exaggerated stories about the precipitating incident being circulated. ("John Jones was shot last night by the Vipers. He didn't even have a chance; he was cornered. They'll pay for this." "The Vipers were in our territory last night messin' with some of our women.")

Tactic: Force the group to go through the process of *reality testing*. Try to pin down the relevant facts exactly: Who, what, where, when and why? These are the important questions:

Who did what? What really happened? Where did it happen? When did it happen? Why would such a thing happen? Who *saw* it? Who did you hear it from? Did he say he saw it with his own eyes? Can he be believed? Is there some reason why he might make up such a story? Why not?

You will probably find that in forcing a test of the reality alleged to be behind the incident you are *introducing a note of skepticism*, deflating the stories that are making the rounds and tending to neutralize them. It is not advisable to hold meetings at this stage of the game. This would only provide an arena where rumors are more effectively circulated and where the Fight forces defend the "integrity" of their view. It is best in this stage to deal with individuals or like-minded cliques within the group. There will be time enough for meeting when and if the group reaches the stage of active planning.

The intermediate phase begins when segments of the group start talking up an attack plan.

Tactic: Suggest a *counter plan* such as having a talk with the leader of the opposing group. Try to arrange a meeting between the Fight-force leaders of the opposing groups. If you succeed in holding such a meeting make sure you are in a position to direct the mediation. A note of caution at this point: although the CYDP staff spent a great amount of time in this kind of mediation, the payoff has not been high. Mediation of this sort (not unlike that which led to the uneasy peace at the 38th parallel in Korea) very often seems to become an end in itself. It can go on and on without resolution. Another warning: do not think too optimistically about achieving a definite *resolution* of gang conflict. Today's incident which appears to have been resolved may be a latent ingredient in tomorrow's battle.

Perhaps the best one can hope for in the short-run approach to gang conflict is the effective stalemate. Our experience has been that *a very high proportion (probably about 90 per cent) of all pro-*

jected gang fights do not occur. We found that most gang fights are halted because of what we will describe as the "Greater Threat" factor. Greater Threat means simply that it is more dangerous to fight than not to fight. It is your job to make everybody aware that this is the case. Usually they already know of the Greater Threat, but it has to be said and your job is to say it—often and loud.

The Greater Threat can take many forms and represents the most important aspect of a group's ability to save face. It may become clear that the opposing gang is superior in numbers, fighting experience, motivation and weapons. Our workers were able to convey successfully the notion that it is smart not to fight when you are assured of defeat.

A more frequent and immediate form of the Greater Threat is the knowledge that the police will know of the impending gang fight and are prepared to deal with it firmly. It was our experience that workers were able to prevent gang fights by conveying in no uncertain terms the police threat to the No-Fight faction of the gang. The police threat has to be elaborated with its consequences of jail, disgrace, interrupted lives, girl friends taking up with other guys, broken-hearted mothers and the like.

Another important factor which the knowledgeable worker may use is the *counter rumor*. There may be talk within the group that the incident which provoked the threat of gang violence "has already been taken care of" (presumably by the police or some other force). Or the talk may be that "we'll take care of this later." Or the worker may be able to convey to the group that if they insist on going into another group's territory and fighting they will have to face the possibility of revenge later; that they will not be able to have peace when they want it; that they will be "jumped" when they want to walk to a candy store or a swimming pool which is located in the territory of an opposing group. It is important for the worker to remind the group of the future consequences of its actions.

In the final phase, if all your efforts have failed and a plan has been formulated which the gang is determined to carry out, you can always call the police. We have had a number of instances in which we told our groups we were calling the police. Our groups have accepted the fact that we will call the police *and have even come to depend upon it.* This has not adversely affected our relations with groups, as might be presumed. They know we are on the side of public order and we do not equivocate about it.

It is not difficult to stop threatened gang fights if you know about the circumstances early enough. Normally we learned of threatened violence a day to a week in advance of the planned battle. The real difficulty is with those fights which develop spontaneously or which the worker stumbles into quite by accident.

In those cases the worker should try to help those youngsters who are trying to stop the fight. He should try to remove the most likely participants from the scene. If the worker has an automobile he may make a quick decision to try to persuade a few of the fighting gang members to get into the automobile and drive out of the troubled area to a point where he can call the police. There are all sorts of possibilities and the individual worker will have to act according to what his analysis of the situation leads him to believe is possible.

Perhaps an account from a report of one of our own workers who encountered a threatening condition will give you the feel for at least one situation:

I patrolled the area. It was raining steadily which gave me cause to be alarmed about a group of about 15 Mexican youths standing on the sidewalk near XXXX W. Taylor Street. After parking the car, I walked toward the gathering. From a distance I saw about four fellows pulling two others apart. Eight of those present were "Gymnastics" (aged 15-17) and Juarez L., a former "Barracuda," Jim "Jungle Jim" S., a former "Gymnastic," some girls, and a couple of neighborhood kids. Six of the "Gymnastics" walked back toward Polk and Laflin streets as Garcia M. and Mario A. stopped to talk to Juarez and Jim. Ignacio A., who was drunk, had walked up to Jim, flipped his neck tie and slugged him in the mouth. Both Garcia and Filipo A. asked the two to forget the incident, that Ignacio was blaming Jimmy S. "for what happened to George A" (about two months ago Juarez L. was provoked into a fight by George A., who was consequently knocked unconscious, largely due to being very high on glue). Juarez L. blew his top: "It was me who kicked his ass—why doesn't he come after me?" I was afraid a fight would ensue because Juarez L.'s remarks were very provoking, but both the "Gymnastics" remained "cool" and left. Jim S. continued to rant and rage: "You don't think I can do it; I can bring coloreds, spics, Italians, from Marshall, Crane [High School], all over—not by the dozens, hundreds, but thousands, millions and burn up this _ _ _ _ ing neighborhood.

Next time I walk the streets, I'll have my uncle's gun, man!" Both began to cool down somewhat as I told them I'm sure they had the good sense not to mess themselves up by "dirtying your hands with fellows who still think it's big to stand on a corner drinking from a bottle!"

Later I saw Garcia M. and Mario A. with their girl friends going east on Taylor. Garcia said he talked to Ignacio who "will forget the whole thing."

Dealing with Potentially
Dangerous Group Situations:
Riots or Mob Actions

AN invariable feature of urban slum communities is a high density of population; that is, there are more people resident in the area than the housing facilities present were originally intended to house. A second feature is a high rate of unemployment of males, especially of young males, who are neither at work nor at school. Thus, whenever weather conditions permit, there are more people on the streets in such areas than in other neighborhoods of the city. Moreover, such areas are usually characterized as having high crime rates and relatively inadequate social and recreational facilities. If all of these negative factors, and still others that have not been mentioned, are combined with some "precipitating incident," the social conditions which exist can trigger some kind of mob action or a riot. Several times during the six-year history of the CYDP our staff was confronted with potentially dangerous group situations. Let us make use of one of these situations as a case study in order to illustrate some general principles of dealing with potentially dangerous group situations.

At the beginning of the 1966 school year the largest high school (predominantly Negro) in one of the areas we served was the scene of a civil-rights demonstration. Leaders of the demonstration marched in protest of what they charged was the unfair and discriminatory firing of a history teacher who had taught at the school for three years. The teacher enjoyed popularity among the many students we interviewed ("He was tough on you, but he made it interesting."). He had been a "permanent substitute" and did not have tenure; like many of the teachers in Chicago's ghetto areas he was temporarily certified. The marchers charged that the teacher

67

had not been invited back to teach in the school in September because he had been a civil-rights activist during the previous summer
(the Chicago school system was viewed by many civil-rights groups
as a major bulwark of racial segregation in the city).

The demonstration took place on one of the hottest days of the
year. It was also the day of school registration; many students were
milling about the front steps of the huge high school (enrollment:
3,500). Some of the leaders of civil-rights groups who were picket-
ing the school building were not known as experienced non-violent
marchers. Our workers reported that the leaders of one of the more
militant of the civil-rights groups seemed to be under the influence
of alcohol as he marched. The demonstration began shortly before
1 P.M. By 2:30 crowds of students had gathered to watch or join in
the marches. People were shouting slogans, singing freedom songs
and the event began in a kind of celebrating mood. Newspapermen,
wire-service reporters, radio and television reporters were on the
scene. The tension was mounting. The marchers not only protested
the alleged dismissal of the history teacher, they also complained
of what they felt were the unfair and insensitive policies of the
white school principal (most of the demonstrators were ignorant of
the fact that the principal had been transferred to another district
on the previous day).

As time passed more students who had been inside the school
registering came out and joined the march or crowds of observers.
More police were sent into the area. Most of the demonstrators were
Negroes. Most of the policemen were white and not familiar with
the area since they were members of a special "Task Force." The
high point of the tension occurred shortly after 3 P.M. when a television camera crew appeared on the scene. The reporter who ac-
companied the camera crew encouraged the marchers to come off the
sidewalk in front of the school where they had been marching in an
orderly fashion and to march in the street for the purpose of
televising a dramatic episode for the evening news program. While
the reporter encouraged the marchers to enter the street (where their
demonstration would be illegal: street marches in Chicago require
permits which must be applied for thirty days in advance—sidewalk
marches do not require a permit) the cameraman complained that

he was not yet ready to film the scene. There was the crowd in the street, impatient to be photographed, eyeing the police who were poised to move in, and appeared to be about to do so, and the reporter, frustrated in his attempts to manipulate a quick crowd scene and get out. Both the crowd and the police began to look provocatively at each other and some cross-talk began that threatened to get out of hand.

Meanwhile, our workers, who were well known in the area and who, in fact, had been helping students register for classes at the school, were busy trying to encourage as many youngsters as possible to leave the scene. They were particularly aware of the empty lot across the street littered with ready-made weapons of broken bottles and bricks (the CYDP that same week had sent a letter to a high-ranking police department official informing him that efficient sanitation in the neighborhood would be a meaningful step toward reducing potential violence in the demonstration area). Our workers would move in with the club's station wagons, entice a load of kids into the vehicle, hightail it out of the area, deposit the kids in their home neighborhood and return for another load.

As it turned out, the reporter finally got his TV shots, the police exercised restraint and control, and persuaded the marchers to return to the sidewalk. Our workers managed to remove some potential trouble-making gang members from the scene and the tension melted away as the march ended at about 4 P.M.

It was out of potential riot situations like this one that we developed the following set of counter-riot techniques which we applied in several other situations. They are presented in a developmental style, as if the potentially dangerous group situation were beginning to develop out of some "precipitating incident," and follow the process of development from stage to stage. It should be clear that if the Counter-Techniques are well carried out at any stage of the process, the Provocative Situations will have been brought under control. Although we never experienced a full-scale riot, we had to deal with several riot-potential situations. The techniques described below have helped to prevent the more dangerous situations from escalating into larger civil disorders.

A Model for Dealing With

Provocative Situations	and	Counter Techniques

Fantastically exaggerated rumors are circulating about some possible precipitating incident. More people are asking "What happened?" than know what happened. Their verbal excitement is what is being communicated.

Counter Rumoring: Deliberately circulate messages which negate the rumors tending to create the riot situation. "Loud-talk" it. In a crowd, just walk up to people and tell them the counter rumor. Plant your counter rumor with people you know will disseminate it.

People are milling about and more people are gathering into a crowd. Some rumors have become more prominent than others and many people now believe they know "the facts." The excitement has gotten people ready for some kind of action and the search for a target or outlet has begun.

Organize a shuttle service with what cars you have and get the people you know out of the area. Circulate in the crowd and advise people to leave the area. Let youngsters who know you be impressed with the fact that you know they are there and can, therefore, identify them. Ask people to help you keep this thing from developing.

The police who are brought into a riot situation are usually strangers to the local people and the area. They may not know the best disposition of their forces in the local area. Most of the time the police have no way of knowing the temper of the crowd until something happens. The more disorderly elements of the crowd are beginning to fix on the police as the most immediate target.

Advise the police. If your advice is sound they may follow your suggestions. Advise the police about "blind spots" in an area, empty lots where bricks may be turned into weapons, or where bottles may be found. Advise the police as to the mood and temper of the crowd. It is vitally important that the police do not assume that a situation is more dangerous than it really is and, conversely, that they do not underestimate the danger in a situation.

Jeering, hollering, hooting and name-calling begins. People begin adopting a provocative posture. The police try to maintain order.

Make use of your counter rumors. "Loud-talk" any and all who may listen. Be and act confident in your knowledge of the real situation. Tell people to "cool it."

Individual aggressions begin and scuffles break out. Some of these are within the crowd itself and some may be directed toward the police.

Break it up yourself, if you have to, by physically separating the scufflers. You can ask some people to be "Pacifiers" and help you keep something dangerous from happening. Warn the scufflers about the danger of arrest and its consequences.

Self-appointed leaders begin urging people to some potentially dangerous course of action.

Become a leader yourself, urging people not to do anything foolish or dangerous. Warn of the consequences.

Polarization is complete. One group of people is now out to hurt another group of people and active aggressive acts on a larger scale are taking place.

The problem is now one for the police and other authorities. If you are well known to *both* the members of the crowd and to the authorities, then you can try to be helpful in preserving life and property. If that is not the case, leave the area for your own safety.

Conducting a Successful Dance
in a High-Delinquency Area

IN working with young people, dances should not simply be conceived of as being only a pleasant diversion. Dances are a relatively formal setting where the sexes can come together in a socially approved manner. As such, dancing is a major form of socialization and can make an important contribution to the social development of youngsters. At the same time, considering the transitional nature of adolescence, and the fact that relatively large numbers of persons of limited acquaintance are brought together in a confined space, dances also include the potential for trouble. This is as true of dances held in a middle-class country club as it is of the average high-school dance in city, town or village, or as it is of dances held in high delinquency inner-city areas. Young men insecure in their masculine competence and young girls ambivalent about their developing femininity are, almost by definition, productive of ambiguous social relations. The social expectations demanding some kind of performance at a dance are apt to differ somewhat for a male among his male friends and for a girl among her girl friends; and these social expectations combined with the possession or absence of skill at dancing, plus the ambivalent attraction of the sexes and the general exuberance of the occasion, make for the kind of approach-avoidance patterns that can result in trouble.

In the early stages of the CYDP, our staff experienced their share of troubles at the dances we organized for street-gang members. Young men "playing" to the male and female audiences we had supplied them, used our dances to disguise their insecurities or incompetence by playing the role of the "tough guy" who might not have the courage or skill to dance but who knew bad language or could throw a punch or two. Similarly, girls testing their attractiveness or seeking to exhibit that they were desirable to partners other than their own, gave rise to competitive relations that resulted in more than dancing. Those with the least confidence in their social competence fortified themselves with drink, either before they had arrived or by secretive drinking during the course of the dance. The high rate of traffic in and out of the dance indicated that some young people had hidden liquor or weapons outside. Altogether, it was clear that control techniques would have to be developed or the dances would have to be abandoned. It simply did not make sense for an anti-delinquency project to provide the resources and occasion for a relatively small number of the youth population to act out a series of "bad man" or "hot babe" performances to the detriment of the positive socializing functions that dances could serve.

Several years of experience of holding dances in high delinquency areas taught us a few things that may be worth passing on to others who may encounter similar problems in the future. It is assumed, as a matter of course, that those who would hold dances in high delinquency areas would address themselves to such questions as the physical safety of the premises to be used and the numerical adequacy of staff to supervise the dance. In what follows we address ourselves to the social-psychological aspects of holding a dance and to specific strategies of control.

Perhaps the two most important general principles we learned about organizing and holding dances—and these principles have much wider application in youth work—are the following: (1) If an activity, like a dance, is to be conducted successfully, both the planning for it, and the activity itself, have to be done *with* the youngsters, not *for* them. The activity must be the result of a real cooperative process in which the opinions and suggestions of young people have been taken seriously, and accepted or rejected on the basis of their debated merits. (2) If those who have the ultimate responsibility for an activity, *i.e.*, the staff and the youth-serving agency, exhibit anxiety about the necessity for controls or their actual application, this will be noted by the youngsters and accepted as a challenge to begin to test limits and to play the game of breaking through the controls. Persons who are overanxious about controls, whether adults or youngsters who have responsibility, should not be maneuvered into positions where their own psychological limitations may contribute to the very situations they seek to prevent.

Conducting a successful dance in a high delinquency area should be conceived of as a process consisting of three distinct phases: the planning and preliminary phase, the dance itself and the close-out and review phase. Each of these phases must be addressed self-consciously with a view to anticipating problems and having techniques and resources at hand to deal with them if they arise.

The youth group or groups in whose name the dance is being held must be told that they are directly and indirectly responsible for everything that happens at the dance. A successful dance will redound to their credit and a dance that results in trouble will be a reflection on their reputation and maturity. In the early stages of discussing responsibilities with the sponsoring youth groups, there will be a tendency for their spokesmen to voice a ready but superficial kind of agreement designed to evade the real issue. They will say, "Yeah, yeah. Sure, anything you say." Suggestions should be made to increase the size and composition of the planning group. A few adults, besides the staff of the agency, should be invited to participate in the discussion and planning for the dance. These adults can be parents, teachers, ministers, youth officers or others. The object of this strategy is to provide a wider audience than merely the youth group itself for the agreements and commitments that are made during the planning phase. Later, these adults as well as the young people who are party to the planning will serve as observers and potential critics for the manner in which the dance is conducted.

The youth group sponsoring the dance must invest time, effort and money toward a successful dance. There must be a division of labor and an allocation of responsibilities and roles to carry out the tasks that precede a dance. Decorations and refreshments must be planned for, tickets have to be devised or printed, music and entertainment must be provided for and the whole process of traffic control, scheduling the events of the evening and money payments must be anticipated. Committees should be formed to carry out specific tasks like purchasing supplies, publicity, ticket sales, decorating the dance hall, traffic and crowd control, and cleanup. Between the time of the initial meeting suggesting the dance and the night of the dance a series of meetings must be anticipated for the planning group as a whole or its various committees. The carrying out of these preliminary tasks brings out internal group tensions and misunderstandings about what is expected of whom. Some of the youngsters will do more and some will do less than they should. Incipient conflicts have to be mediated through active supervision of the series of meetings that report on the progress of activities. During these meetings the staff and the leaders of the youth group must constantly reaffirm the agreements and commitments made in earlier planning meetings so that roles and responsibilities are clear. It may even be necessary to reassign some roles and tasks because youngsters have promised more than they can deliver. Despite an atmosphere of crisis as the night of the dance approaches, if the planning and communication during the preliminary phase has been adequate the potential for trouble has already been reduced.

An essential final step that should not be overlooked is advance notification to the police and other interested social agencies about the date and time of the dance. Ordinarily the police will arrange to have their squad cars make more frequent runs along the streets most heavily traveled by the youngsters as they come to the dance and at the time they leave. This kind of police surveillance when well-managed will be casual and informal so that it may even go unnoticed if all goes well. The police can also be asked to have a man in plain-clothes drop in to the dance from time to time in the course of the evening, or a youth officer in plain-clothes may be assigned to cover the dance in an informal manner. Other agencies in the area should be notified in order to avoid conflicts in schedules and so they can account for fluctuations in attendance at their own activities.

Traffic and crowd control, as youngsters arrive at the dance or leave when it is over, must be provided for in advance. The best known and most socially adept youngsters should be on the reception committee in order to serve gatekeeping functions. Near the entrance to the hall, and placed so that it cannot be avoided, there should be a reception table with a guest booth where tickets are taken and where all who attend are signed in. The names and addresses entered in the guest book should be verified from some kind of identification that the youngsters are asked to present. Not all youngsters will be able to supply identification, especially the younger ones; their identity should be vouched for by someone who knows them and the latter's name should be entered in the guest book along with the name of the youngster he identified. Unidentifiable strangers who cannot be vouched for should not be admitted to the dance. Barring a youngster from the dance can contain the seed for trouble so the matter must be handled diplomatically and explained in terms of prior agreements made during the planning phase for the dance.

Hats and outer-coats should be checked at some distance from the entrance or exit. Youngsters are less likely to "hit and run" if they have to leave something behind. Two or three socially adept youngsters should have been assigned the role of circulating crowd controllers who keep an eye on the dancers and step in quickly to prevent trouble. Going in and out of the dance should be discouraged. Since everything essential to the dance is on the inside— music, refreshments, companions and toilet facilities—there should be no excuse for leaving unless one is leaving for good. Despite an agreed rule: "once out, stay out," there may be some traffic in and out. These are the youngsters that may require special surveillance. Sometimes a "wise guy" has hidden a bottle of liquor outside and he or others may try to get to it and return; or someone has "gotten mad" and is going out for a weapon. Youngsters who leave and return must be detained when they return in order to determine whether they have been drinking or if they exhibit impatience and hostility—signs of anger. If a youngster smells of liquor, acts drunk, or if he will not submit to search upon reasonable suspicion that he might have a concealed weapon, he should be forbidden re-entry. In the latter case, it may also be advisable to call for some reinforcements. In any of these cases where the potential for trouble is high, it is important for the order-keepers to be polite but firm and perfectly clear.

If, through some happenstance, trouble should start, the circulating crowd controllers and the staff should get the youngsters involved away from the dance area as quickly as possible. This may be done by verbal appeals for order but, if necessary, the troublemakers should be physically "hauled" off the dance floor. Speed is essential because excitement is contagious and can set off a chain reaction. Simultaneously, while the incident is still in the "what's happening" stage for most of the crowd, the members of the sponsoring group and the staff must label the incident and "talk it down." The incident should be labeled—stupid, silly, dumb, a minor incident that is already over, or an incident that is unworthy of notice. Meanwhile the crowd controllers and the staff can deal with the participants to the incident in a nearby room or office and decide what needs to be done on the merits of what can be learned.

About half an hour before the dance is officially over the closing time of the dance should be announced between dance numbers. This will prepare the crowd for the end of the dance and will tend to space-out traffic as some of the dancers leave early. It is important to reduce the type of "bunching" that takes place at the checkroom and the front door because pushing and shoving can lead to escalation. The local police station should be phoned and the desk sergeant reminded that the dance will be over in half an hour. This will give him time to alert nearby squad cars that can exercise informal surveillance along the main routes away from the dance.

As the youngsters leave the dance, arrangements should be made to escort home one or another of the dancers who may require an escort for whatever reason. There will usually be a few such youngsters in any crowd. The clean-up committee should go to work to put the dance facility into reasonable order for the night, with a view to returning the next day for a more thorough job of restoring the place to its pre-dance condition.

A few members of the sponsoring youth group and members of the agency staff should get together for a short review of the events of the evening. The planning and conduct of the dance should be discussed in terms of what went off well or ill and how future dances may enhance their chances for greater success. The guest list should be reviewed in order to identify any problem cases during the process of identification, at the cloakroom, during the course of the dance, entering and leaving and at close-out time. During the course of this discussion the staff should praise everyone who made positive contributions toward the success of the dance and encourage members of the sponsoring group to "talk to" young people who may have misbehaved. If money was charged for ticket sales before the dance and/or at the door, there should be a public accounting of receipts and the money placed in responsible hands. Finally, a staff member should phone the police and thank them for their services to the dance.

Informal Counseling Techniques
for Individuals and Groups

PERHAPS one of the most universal generalizations about so-called hard-to-reach youth is that they are *not hard to reach;* rather, they may be *hard to work with* after they have been reached. What this means is that it is first necessary to establish a relationship with youngsters and then to have a method to use that relationship to some constructive end. The principal ingredient in our street work and community organization program, our method of working with youngsters, was mainly talk. This informal counseling was a part of our program to achieve the project's action goals of changing the behavior of individuals and groups, helping them to meet their needs for association, friendship and status and helping youngsters to prepare themselves for adult roles by providing information and guidance.

We did not have a clinic where "clients" were seen according to appointments and schedules. We soon learned that most of the young people we worked with, at least in the earlier stages of our relationship to them, were not trained in the middle-class habits of clock-watching, writing down dates and giving priority to mutual agreements. Instead, we felt it was our responsibility to arrange matters in such a way that counseling opportunities would become almost unavoidable. Counseling opportunities, therefore, became a natural by-product of the fact of association no matter where or when such association between youngsters and workers might take place. The two principal settings for this kind of talk, or informal counseling, were the Outpost and the station wagon, whose functions have been discussed elsewhere.

In short, we counseled youngsters when and where we could, and the opportunities for such counseling were far more numerous than might be expected. Counseling sessions are, of course, best conducted in privacy, but the notion of privacy is a relative thing. We soon learned that sufficient privacy for the discussion of many kinds of problems can be created at the most unlikely times and places, for example, by going off to the side and talking quietly, even in the midst of a dance or a sports event.

Once a relationship had been established, our workers did not find it difficult to talk to young people, even about relatively personal or intimate matters. They did not have to be aggressive to get youngsters to respond to informal conversation. As a matter of fact, boys and girls often took the initiative, even though they might be indirect or be asking on behalf of "a friend." At such times as the worker opened up the subject by telling a youngster he wanted to talk to him about something, the response of the youngster was usually positive. Most of the time young people seemed to regard it as natural and normal that a worker should want to discuss such personal questions as: (1) I understand you have been expelled from school. (2) Why were you picked up by the police the other night? (3) Are you really planning to marry the girl you "knocked up"? (4) Your mother tells me you haven't been home the past two nights. (5) Did you quit your job or get fired? (6) Joe Smith tells me you owe him four dollars. (7) What was that you were drinking out of a paper bag outside? (8) How come we don't see your friend Jimmy around any more? (9) Why is it that I never see you carrying books home from school? (10) Is it true that you are "out to get" Frankie; why?

There were, of course, young people who did not want to talk or take part, either individually or as a group, in counseling or informal talk. These youngsters would use "ploys" to stop the talk and we developed "counter ploys" which frequently started it up again. Here are some examples of "ploys" and "counter ploys."

Ploy	*Counter Ploy*
"I don't want to talk about that crap."	"Let's talk about why you don't want to talk about it."
"I don't know nothing about that stuff."	"Yes, you do. You just don't know you know about it."

Ploy	Counter Ploy
"Who cares?"	"Let's ask everybody here and find out who cares."
"You're always trying to get us to talk about something. What are you up to anyway?"	"What do you think I'm up to?"
(Silence!)	"Why is everything so quiet all of a sudden?"

These counter ploys were especially useful in encouraging groups to begin informal discussions. We were able to turn many of these informal group discussions into teaching and learning experiences. After a while we began to label them "didactic bull sessions." For example, a group of boys are with a worker in a station wagon and are just riding around the city. They drive through a neighborhood drastically different from the one in which they live. The people in the area are well dressed. They live in neat, clean, higher-income homes. The homes are set back on tree-lined lots. The boys begin to notice things like bikes being left unguarded in front of those homes. All of these things are points of departure for informal counseling as soon as the subject can be opened up.

The worker takes this opportunity to point out why this neighborhood is the way it is. He asks questions and focuses on the youngsters' perceptions of the neighborhood. The worker forces elaboration. How much do those houses cost? Where do the people who live around here work? What do you have to do to get a job like they have? What kind of education would that job require? If you made that much money would you keep part of it in a bank? Would you invest it? Would you still have to maintain credit and charge things? And, why wasn't that bike locked up?

Almost any situation can be turned into a didactic bull session of this type. Casual remarks made about girls passing by can be turned into discussions of the relations between the sexes and their consequences, marriage, the family, planning for the future and how to achieve it. We also held many didactic bull sessions on such problems as employment, military service, school, the condition of the neighborhood, politics, and race relations.

In both group and individual counseling our workers were generally trained to use two methods. The first which will be described here, is derived from Anatol Rappaport's *Fights, Games and Debates.*

Our workers were encouraged to view themselves as "change agents." This does not mean that they did the changing that needed to be done, but rather that they precipitated the kinds of change in viewpoint on the part of others which enabled those others to proceed with their own self-formulated change programs. It is this matter of *viewpoint* that is the keystone of Rappaport's technique. That is, according to Rappaport, a person cannot change the way he acts unless he changes the way he looks at things. He must alter his images of reality. The process of making this kind of change, however, is threatening and, in trying to get youngsters to obtain new perspectives on themselves and their problems, our workers were encouraged to use techniques which reduced the degree of threat involved in looking at life in new ways.

First our workers tried to assure the youngster being counseled that he was being heard and that he was being understood. Second, the worker was careful to make it known that he regarded the youngster's thinking or viewpoint as valid and meaningful. And third, the worker did his best to demonstrate that an area of similarity existed between the worker's view and the view of the young man being counseled. All of these positive reassurances are the necessary pre-conditions to make the youngster receptive to change. The worker then outlines for the young man the areas of difference between their positions, always granting the boy his right to his position and emphasizing the degree of validity that it includes. We found that if the young man was persuaded at all he was persuaded *by the facts* as the worker presented them; he was not persuaded by some sentimental regard for the worker. It was the worker's job to present the truth, gently and clearly, and let truth do the persuading.

We also made extensive use of another method taught at the National Training Laboratories at Bethel, Maine. Again, the technique focused on helping the other by working with him to clarify his own situation. Our workers almost always proceeded in the interrogative mode. They asked questions designed to reveal the most appropriate course of action. Our workers assumed that they did not necessarily know what needed to be done. They assumed instead that they and the youths they worked with were involved in a joint project, in a search for relevant truth. The earliest model of this form of counseling is the Socratic method as presented in the works of Plato.

The NTL technique begins with a most important question that the worker needs to raise in every counseling situation: Who has the problem? A problem may be concerned with the relations between the Self, an Other, a Group, an Organization, a Community, or Society.

It is necessary for the worker to try to make this clear for the youngster so that both the youngster and the worker know who it is that has to be dealt with or considered. In other words, the point to be determined is where do you gain entry? If a boy has a problem with his girl friend you cannot do much about it by talking about society's role in the affair because it is not likely that you can change society to help the boy and his girl solve their problem, at least in the short run. So it is really a question of, who sees the situation as a problem? Those who see it as a problem are the ones who can work on it.

The second question the worker needs to raise is, what is the nature of the problem? Problems can be problems of: (1) Communication (2) Energy (3) Reality awareness (4) Goals (5) Means (6) Skills.

Problems, of course, usually combine several of the above factors. With a boy and his girl, for example, the problem may be one of communication and reality awareness. The problem of a youngster who has dropped out of school could involve factors of communication, energy, reality awareness, goals, means and skills. So we tried to start at the point of least resistance in counseling a boy with complex problems. And that meant we frequently started at the entry points of reality awareness and communication. If, for example, a worker saw that a youngster's problem of unemployment was a function of his lack of skills, the worker brought this into the boy's reality awareness and put him into contact with various programs which could help train the boy; thereby providing him with the means for the attainment of his goals.

These techniques can readily be adopted by anybody at almost any time or place. In the group counseling or bull session it is possible to get young people themselves to take part in the elaboration process that the worker normally would initiate himself in individual counseling. We would ask boy "A" what he thought about a problem and then ask boy "B" what he thought about what boy "A" had said. Everyone present would then begin to look for contrasts and contradictions which would help develop the needed elaboration. Our workers always tried to turn these group sessions into discussions rather than arguments, while they acted as mediators of the debate. In most instances of group and individual counseling it has been our experience that young men and women want to talk and, given the opportunity, they will do so.

Language Training Through Games

WE had perceived the necessity for trying to change the way most of our contact kids used the English language before we became aware of the work of Frank Reissman, Martin P. Deutsch and Basil Bernstein, but these three social scientists helped us crystallize our own thinking on the importance of language training.

Reissman, Deutsch, Bernstein and others have pointed out that the lower-class child is especially disadvantaged in school because he has had little experience in the use of that "language code" which is "the language code of the school." The lower-class child speaks what Bernstein calls *a restricted code*. The restricted code is "characterized by a reduction in qualifiers, adjectives, adverbs, particularly those which qualify feelings, the organization of the speech is comparatively simple, there is a restriction on the use of the self-referent pronoun I, and an increase in personal pronouns."

Reissman in an article entitled "Are the Deprived Non-Verbal?" points to some of the findings of the Institute for Developmental Studies:

1. Deprived children appear to be poor in the use of verbs but much better with descriptive adjectives.
2. Deprived children seem to understand more language than they speak (their receptive linguistic ability is much better than their expressive language).
3. Deprived children demonstrate a surprising ability for phantasy.
4. Deprived children express themselves best in spontaneous, unstructured situations.

It was our belief that a kid who could speak only in the restricted code was severely disadvantaged in every area of life where he has to interact with people who do not speak, and even look down on those who speak, in restricted codes. We, therefore, looked for ways of teaching our contacts the more formal codes of English. Professor Higgins had the same problem with Eliza Doolittle in "My Fair Lady."

Richard Booze, one of our extension workers, was especially active and inventive in the area of language training. Some of his techniques included the following:

1. *The Challenge:* Kids were challenged to "make a speech" for 2 or 3 minutes spontaneously, on a specific topic, using proper grammar and pronunciation, and without repeating themselves. The challenge was always made in the presence of an audience and was turned into a competitive game. Topics were picked by the challenger, were usually humorous, and were suggested by something that happened recently.

2. *Corrective Feedback:* If a kid made a particularly egregious error in grammar or pronunciation, the worker repeated what had been said, but in correct form, and playfully refused to continue the discussion until the kid had corrected his error by repeating what the worker had said. For example, our kids would frequently say "Where it at?" The worker would respond: "Behind the preposition." The confusion created by the worker's answer could then be turned into a grammar lesson.

3. *Role Playing:* Kids were instructed to use correct speech and grammar in a role play and then to change roles and speak in slang. The worker would role play a person responding to the kid and demonstrate in his role how people react to different styles of speech. Some of the roles played by the worker were teacher, employer, policeman, judge, and adults generally.

4. *Role Model:* By speaking in the formal code himself, in his interaction with kids, the worker provided an example of how to speak. This by itself is not enough but it is one way of teaching, and kids do learn from it.

5. *Substitution:* The workers frequently used polysyllabic terms

for common slang terms such as: bread, cool, dig, jazz, pad, crib, rank, sound, and so on. For example, a worker would say, "He's very nonchalant. That means cool." "I doubt his veracity. That means I think he's jiving you." This was done with tongue in cheek and became a kind of game in itself.

6. *Bull Sessions:* In bull sessions the workers frequently brought up the topic of speech and emphasized the different ways in which a person can speak, and how other people may react to different ways of speaking.

Our goal was not to get our kids to stop speaking in restricted code but, rather, to expand their restricted code into the formal codes of the English language. We found that our contact kids were very interested in learning new words and new ways of saying things. We kept dictionaries around the Outpost to settle arguments.

We feel, as a result of our experience, that much more time and deliberation should be given to work on language than we were able to give. This is an extremely important area of work with youngsters and a great deal more effort should be devoted to helping inner city kids improve the way they speak.

Role Playing

ROLE playing, as a human relations training technique, has been developed largely by the National Training Laboratories. Role playing is based to a considerable extent on the theoretical work of Mead and Cooley.

Mead postulated that human interaction resembles nothing so much as a game in that any human interaction involves the taking of roles. The taking or playing of one's role assumes knowledge of the roles of all the players involved. In baseball, for example, the pitcher and the catcher have their respective, separate, roles but their ability to play together is based upon their understanding of each other's roles. Simply stated, the pitcher knows what the catcher is likely to do and the catcher knows what the pitcher is likely to do. It is this mutually shared knowledge of mutual expectations which makes the game possible. Everyone knows the rules and everyone knows his role.

Knowledge of the rules and the roles of all of the participants in the game, taken together, constitutes the "generalized other" which is incorporated into the "Self." A self can function adequately to the extent to which its knowledge of the generalized other is correct. Efficiency in human relations is relative to the degree of awareness and precision of knowledge that the self has regarding the generalized other. Where this knowledge is deficient and imprecise, or the relations between Self and Other are characterized by hostility and rejection, we have disorganization, both personal and social.

Cooley's concept of the "looking-glass self" grows out of his reflections on the "primary group." The primary group is characterized by face-to-face interaction, we-feeling, and inclusion. Humans derive their sense of self from the groups of which they are members. It is others who tell us who we are. The primary group is literally a mirror in which one's self is reflected back to one. We know who we are because we are told who we are, and we are told who we are by the members of our primary groups. Our primary groups are composed of significant others from whom we learn our sense of self. By taking the role of the other we become human and we are human to the extent that we can take the role of the other.

Role playing can be viewed as a way of training people to be effectively human. It ties into and taps within us our most fundamental human beingness. Our contact boys might have expressed it as, "That's where it's at."

We found no difficulty in getting kids to understand role playing. There is some initial shyness but it is easily overcome by having the worker do some role plays himself or with one other. Role plays themselves can begin with the simple and brief and work up gradually to the complex and long. Even inanimate objects can be used as an other. A chair, for example, can play the role of teacher while a boy explains something to "him" or "her." Roles can be written up or played out spontaneously. The same goes for plots. You can, for example, say to a boy, "I'll play a policeman who just told you to get off this corner. You be yourself. We'll play it through once where you come on strong. Then we'll switch and you be the policeman and I'll come on soft and cool. Everybody else here can be the audience and tell us how we're doing when we're through." Everyone present at a role-play session should be involved, either as player or as observer, with assigned tasks.

We used role playing in training youth in relating to employers, teachers, friends, girls, police and so on. So far as we can tell the youth with whom we tried it enjoyed it and learned something. We did not use role playing to help kids learn how to manipulate the other. Somehow it turns out that efficiency in human relations is "doing unto the other as you would have the other do unto you."

The Gang-Up

THE number of boys who need the services of an out-reach worker vastly outnumber the supply of competent youth workers available. Therefore, a worker usually counsels a group, several groups or, at least, an individual. One would not, ordinarily, expect to see two or three workers simultaneously concentrating on the problems of just one boy.

And yet that is exactly what we did in the cases of special boys with special problems. We tossed aside the rigid concept of man-power hours spent per boy and developed a special counseling technique we call the "gang-up." In the gang-up two or three workers get together with a "special" boy and give him "the treatment." It can be positive treatment that builds up the boy's ego and reinforces his current good behavior, or it can be negative treatment—a dressing-down or calling to account for undesirable behavior.

The practice of ganging-up is not an entirely new concept. In many areas of society, from the office to the locker room, the gang-up is an unconscious style of communication that is quite commonplace.

A salesman in a large company suddenly finds himself surrounded by two or three executives of his firm in an office. These executives "go to work" on him in a good-natured way:

"Charlie, now that you've finally scored with an account, maybe *you'll* buy the drinks."

"You know, Charlie, I hate to admit it, but I was going around the office spreading the nasty rumor that you were too good a golfer to be any kind of a salesman."

"Charlie, congratulations. For a guy who wears the kind of ties you wear, you gotta be great to sell anything to anybody."

The executives may not know it, but they have just ganged up in a friendly, kidding, positive way on their pal Charlie.

In work with boys with negative problems or positive potential

89

the appearance of the gang-up should be just as casual. But in reality a good gang-up on a boy is carefully planned.

The first requirement of a good gang-up is a thorough knowledge of the boy they will be counseling by the workers. A boy, in his own knowing way, must also be prepared for a gang-up. To go back to our example of Charlie the salesman—if he had just learned of the death of a good friend and his executive friends did not know of this when they ganged-up on him, their encouragement would have been seriously out of place. So it is important that before workers "gang-up" on a boy that they make some tactful inquiries of him and his friends in order to know what is happening in his life.

To a certain extent the workers should define what it is they want to accomplish in a gang-up. They should work out a rough plan of attack: who will say what and when.

A gang-up should be conducted from beginning to end with as little outside interruption as possible. The location can range from the workers' office to a station wagon ride.

In any case, it is best to isolate the boy in some way so that concentrated, multiple and simultaneous focusing of attention on him can proceed without interruption.

Our gang-ups had three purposes:

1. To bring a boy back into a desired line of behavior.
2. To encourage him to continue in a desirable pattern of conduct.
3. To help prepare him for an important future task or responsibility.

Our closed-door gang-ups developed into highly explicit, intensive "feedback" sessions. It is important to note the dramatic difference in roles in a gang-up: here is a boy who usually views himself, and thinks, perhaps, he is viewed by others, only as a part of a larger group (the street gang or club). He may previously have seen the worker only in company with several boys or with a number of groups. Now *he* alone, is surrounded by two or three workers. It can be a traumatic event in his life.

Generally speaking, the gang-up consists of either positive or negative feedback. On the positive side, the gang-up can be likened to everything from a pep talk, to a psychological transfusion of values, to a vaccination or booster shot, or ego creation. The gang-up is used on boys who have strong leadership capabilities, or who show promise of developing such leadership, with the intention of encouraging them to use their talents and influence in pro-social activities and attitudes.

For example, the workers may have decided that a young gang leader whom we shall call "Dale" deserves a gang-up commendation not only to encourage him to finish high school with high enough grades to qualify for a junior-college scholarship, but also to motivate him to try to help fellow members of his gang develop a sense of urgency about performing well in school. Here is how that gang-up went once the young man found himself alone with two workers in a club room:

Worker A: "Hey, Dale, am I glad you finally found time to honor us with your presence at the club tonight. I am *mighty* glad because I was over at Central High this afternoon on some business when who did I run into but the great James McQuade Jones, your English teacher. He said so many nice things about you I had to blush, and for me that isn't easy."

(Dale is standing, looking at the floor, a little nervous and grinning with unconcealed glee.)

Worker B: "Yeah, that's pretty sweet news because I know James McQuade Jones too, and he's got to be the toughest, meanest, best old English teacher Central ever had. And if *you* are causin' him to say nice things about you, then you must be as smart as I've been sayin' you are all along."

Worker A: "You know, Dale, the important thing to us about the good work you've been doing this year, not only in school but also here at the club, is that there seem to be so darn many times when we put faith in a guy; we hear pretty good things about him and we try to help him and then he lets us down. You haven't been a let-down guy, and when you get that scholarship next spring it'll be because you've had the good sense to hit the books instead of the street corners."

Worker B: "That's right, old man. Say, do you still want to be a teacher?"

Dale: "I think so."

Worker B: "Well, I hope you can start early because I'm telling you, if some of your buddies don't wise up and start followin' your example they're going to wind up out in the street lookin' for day labor. Man, we sure are countin' on you to help us with those guys. OK?"

Dale: "Yeah, sure. I'll try."

The workers continued to compliment Dale. His accomplishments and his attitude were met with repeated enthusiastic approval. And the workers continued to lay expectations on him; "We know you can do it," and "This ought to be easy for a guy like you."

There are a number of variations of the positive gang-up technique which can be employed on others than the top gang leaders. We used the gang-up with boys who seemed to have become apathetic because of some combination of frustrating circumstances. We found that a psychological transfusion of praise, support and encouragement often helped to counteract these frustrations; that we were able to unfreeze the boy and get him moving again.

We employed the gang-up on boys who had made a promising start in a new and worthy direction but who had gotten sidetracked temporarily because of a passing frustrating experience. In these instances, the gang-up served as a sort of booster at a vulnerable time. And we found that we needed to use the gang-up as general supportive counseling. If we learned nothing else on this project it was that boys who are doing well in generally adverse circumstances *should never be taken for granted.* We used the gang-up on them when time and resources permitted because we felt they deserved on-going encouragement to reinforce their commendable behavior.

The negative gang-up can be likened to everything from an "inquisition" to ego destruction. But even when the form and content of the gang-up are negative in orientation, we conducted it within a positive framework, with a constructive end in view. We did not simply criticize the boy and leave him with a series of negative images about himself. Whatever criticisms we made of him were made in such a way as to express liking, concern and interest in his future welfare. We did this through the use of humor, gentle irony and invidious comparisons that left a basis for a positive relationship in the future. Constructive suggestions were always included in the negative gang-ups.

We used the negative gang-up on boys who demonstrated undesirable leadership, on those who instigated trouble through their influence on others, and on those who were influenced by negative leadership or an adverse set of circumstances. Our workers criticized these boys in terms of what they were doing to themselves, their families and their friends. The workers, in seeking to encourage a change in a boy's behavior, would clearly articulate the consequences of continuing in the negative direction. These consequences were followed out to their conclusion and the worst alternatives at every choice point in the future were included. We reviewed everything that contributed to the boy's negative image; his actions, dress, language, attitudes and response to criticism. We were careful to also express great concern for the boy's future so that our criticism would not just alienate him. We did not want to reject the boy because we knew that he would simply "reject his rejectors" and the relationship would be lost beyond hope for constructive influence.

In our example of the negative gang-up, two workers have noticed that a gang member we shall call "Eddy" has been truant from school and has been involved in several skirmishes on the street. Here is how that gang-up went once Eddy found himself alone in the club room with the two workers:

Worker A: "Eddy, I suppose you think that when I saw you here earlier tonight, I thought everything was OK and it's all grins. You haven't been here for three weeks but now you think you'll just slink back to the clubhouse and pretend like nothing happened and nobody missed you. Brother, I don't know who you are trying to kid."

Worker B: "He probably thinks we don't know anything about what's been happening at school and that we would welcome him with open arms tonight. Eddy, dear old Eddy, has come back to our clubhouse. Big deal. Dear old Eddy is lucky he isn't doin' time in County Jail tonight."

Worker A: "That might not be such a bad idea. They have a school in the basement of the jail and I understand that most of the goof-offs who are servin' time over there are required to attend classes every day. It's a cinch that our Eddy isn't inclined to go to class unless he's forced. Right, Eddy?"

Eddy: (head down, sweating) "No. That ain't right."

Worker A: (mocking him) " 'No. That ain't right.' Can't you speak better English than that?"

Eddy: "Yes, sir."

Worker B: "You know, Eddy, you let us down this fall. Remember those fine intentions about school you expressed last summer? Remember all the talks about school we had?"

Eddy: "Yes, sir."

Worker A: "You not only let us down, but you let your mother down. She's trying to earn enough bread to keep your family alive and what do you do? You goof-off out in the street; pushin' old winos around if they don't come up with a bottle. You're just damn lucky you guys weren't caught Thursday. I know all about that incident. And your mother is worried sick. You haven't been home for three days."

Worker B: "And what about your younger brothers? What do you think they think of you? Huh?"

Eddy: "I don't know."

Worker B: "I'll say you don't know. You don't know anything. But you think you know everything. You're becoming a wise guy. But you know what disappoints me, Eddy? Not just that you let us down at the club, not just that you let your mother and your brothers down, but you really are letting yourself down. I thought of you as a guy who respected himself enough to keep the promises you made not only to us but to yourself."

Worker A: "That's the way I feel. We wouldn't raise so much Cain about you, Eddy, if you didn't know any better. You know better, but something's got to be buggin' you. We can't help you if you won't come around the clubhouse for three weeks. What's been happenin', fellow? What's your trouble?"

The workers now concentrate on trying to help Eddy. They have given him a dressing-down; they follow up with a probing of his troubles and some constructive suggestions for how he can get along better in school.

The gang-up does not seem to alienate kids. In fact, it seems to strengthen the out-reach worker-boy relationship. When properly conducted, even a negative gang-up does not leave hard feelings on the part of boys who have been subjected to it. The main elements that preserve relationships between workers and boys are the positive expressions of concern for the boys and the humor that is mixed into the criticism. On the basis of a good deal of experience with this technique, it seems to us that kids who have been exposed to it do change their behavior for the better or maintain good conduct. Even the failures are interesting because they fail after a sincere attempt to change. In the case of failures the technique is continued along with other measures designed to influence conduct.

Stake Animals

THERE is a certain conceit in sending an out-reach worker into the community to establish relationships with gangs and to expect with confidence that he will exert influence over them in one direction; that is, without them, in turn, influencing him. This is especially true when the worker is a relatively young man with a relatively middle-class set of values and the youth group is a delinquent gang reflecting not only a lower-class set of values but a definite leaning toward the antisocial and criminal opportunities afforded by a deprived or exploited community. Such a set of relationships, in such a context, is fraught with all kinds of ambiguous possibilities. The most obvious possibility is the one that has probably never happened, at least it is outside our realm of experience, and that is that the worker goes over to the other side, so to speak, and joins the gang. The possibility of corrupting the worker is not, however, limited to the constant testing of his motives toward venality. The possibilities are numerous. Among the more seductive modes of corrupting the worker are those that fix upon his impulses toward generosity, humanitarianism and sentimentality, as well as those that play upon his desire to elicit conventional responses from his gang-member clients. After two years of observing the interaction between workers and the members of more than forty different youth groups, it seemed to us that the problem of corruption through sentimentality was of sufficient frequency and magnitude to call for a serious review of our work methods.

It was repeatedly observed in the field, and reflected in the daily activity reports of the workers, that in working with a youth group of perhaps eight to fifteen members, too many of our workers had become too deeply involved and over-committed with a particular kind of boy who seldom evidenced any positive behavioral changes despite the excessive efforts devoted toward helping him. Such an application of the workers' time and talent tended to reduce what should have been group-work methods to a species of private case work with one boy, while the behavior and needs of the remaining group members, who were present, went relatively unobserved and unaddressed.

A special investigation of several such boys, who seemed to have an overweening fascination for the worker, revealed that they tended to share some common characteristics. They were the ones who were really problem-laden. The social pattern from which they emerged and the personality type that they tended to exhibit, were strikingly similar in most cases. Their families were broken or highly disorganized, or both. Drunken fathers and mothers with quick tempers and violent methods of discipline, crowded home situations, grinding poverty, dependence on relief and rejection of the boy, rounded out the picture. The boy himself was either a school drop-out or a frequent truant who was even more frequently expelled. He had a history of delinquency, drank to excess when he got the chance and had no real inclination to work. On top of it all, more frequently than not, he freely related all his problems to anyone who would listen, especially the worker.

We came to label such boys "Stake Animals." The term comes from big-game hunting and refers to an injured or helpless animal that is staked out to lure unsuspecting quarry. As ordinarily conceived, and to stay within the bounds of the metaphor, in out-reach work the worker is usually considered the hunter and the delinquent gang, or at least its delinquent tendencies, are his legitimate quarry. In the case of our use of the term, however, the hunter became the prey. The stake animal's many delinquent and dependent characteristics diverted the worker's attention from his legitimate concern, the group, and entrapped most of his time, energy and resources. What was so seductive about the stake animal to the worker was that he seemed to be almost rotten-ripe with the musk of potential reform. At least, that seemed to be the way in which the worker perceived the stake animal for a considerable period of time before disillusion or demoralization set in.

The role of the stake animal vis-à-vis the worker and the rest of the group was also important. At first it seemed to us that there was a conspiracy on the part of the group to push the stake animal off on the worker, to keep him happy and occupied. While this may have been true in some cases, the situation was really more complex. What seemed to occur was a three-way "deception" based on an inadequate appreciation of the degree to which a worker could be helpful to a stake-animal type of boy. Sometimes the gang members would actively solicit the worker's attention and focus it on the one whom they knew, better than anyone else, needed the most help. Sometimes the gang members seemed to do the same thing out of cynical motives, in order to exploit the worker. At all times it seemed to us, at least in our preliminary analysis, that the worker was self-deceived by seriously entertaining the notion that he was going to have any positive and lasting effect on a stake animal. After all, the type of boys we came to label as stake animals had such deep-seated and longstanding problems that only the most highly qualified kind of professional help seemed to be capable of making the fundamental changes required.

Regardless of the motives of the parties involved, however, the objective situation, and the constructive possibilities, of the relation between the worker and the stake animal seemed very unpromising. The objective situation was that when the out-reach worker first came on the scene and began to invest time, energy and resources in cultivating a relationship to the group, the stake animal of that group, if it included one, welled to the surface and a binding tie was established with the worker, while all the others in the group exploited this relationship. The other members of the gang were thus enabled to enjoy all the benefits of having a relationship with a worker without getting caught in the reciprocity of human relations which is the coin of the realm in street work. While the worker was pre-occupied with the stake animal the other members of the group did not feel they had been placed under any obligation to the worker and thus he was in no position to place demands upon them for conforming behavior. They were not even inconvenienced to the extent of having to try to prevent him from intervening in their lives, except at times of their own choosing, for he was hopelessly engulfed by the many problems of the stake animal.

The occasions upon which this seeming neutralization of the

worker's efforts were most readily observable were in situations of limited mobility. For example, we noticed that when the worker took the members of a group for a ride in a car and there was a stake animal in the group, he almost invariably occupied the front seat next to the worker. For the duration of the ride then, the worker's attention, except for his driving, was focused on the stake animal. The worker elicited an endless procession of problems. He advised, counseled, made suggestions and only addressed the rest of the group in the car when absolute necessity required him to reduce the pandemonium. Similarly, when the worker was just "hanging around" with a group, when no structured activity was going on, the worker was soon found engaged in prolonged sessions of one-to-one counseling with a stake animal instead of distributing his attention over the entire group.

Most of the worker's time spent with such a boy was taken up with eliciting promises of reform, almost none of which were kept. At best the stake animal was a short-run reformist and usually he was a classical backslider and recidivist. In fact, we found that the amount of time spent with a stake animal was negatively related to the degree of influence the worker held over him, and it was not an unreasonable inference that backsliding was the stake animal's very technique for preserving his relationship to the worker.

Despite these repeated frustrations, it was our observation that the workers' attraction to the stake animals remained strong. In fact, the personal humanitarian challenge to try to reform such boys, or at least to do something for them, tended to override the supervisory pressures placed on the workers to spread their time, energy and resources over a larger number of the boys we counseled. In short, the workers' attachment to the stake animals seemed to constitute as much of a problem to those supervising the workers as the boys' behavior constituted a problem to the workers. More important, from the standpoint of the effective use of manpower and resources, the uneconomic concentration of effort on what seemed to be the cases least amenable to change, when the objective of the action programs was to have a mass effect, seemed to be a self-defeating enterprise. Such was our state of mind when we were about to make some serious revisions in our out-reach work program, but further research revealed that *the stake animal had some positive latent functions that made him a useful animal, indeed.* In fact, we found that under certain conditions it was more profitable to maintain the relationship between the worker and the stake animal in order to achieve a more widespread effect on our target population. (See chapter on "The Constructive Use of a Stake Animal: The Sounding Board.")

The Constructive Use of a Stake Animal: The Sounding Board

OUR experiences in trying to help the stake-animal kind of boy at first seemed to indicate that our workers had been entrapped by the very kind of youngster they were least likely to be able to help. Certain boys, as you will recall, came to be referred to as "stake animals" because their many serious problems were a seduction to the humanitarian impulse of out-reach workers. As a result, it was the worker who was trapped, rather than his quarry, the problem-laden delinquent boy. Repeated attempts on the part of the worker to help such boys simply resulted in no visible positive accomplishment. It seemed, therefore, that the best policy decision to be made was to abandon such boys and to invest our energies in those that seemed to hold more promise as candidates for change or reform. A little research, however, on the nature of the relationship between workers, stake animals and other members of the group, revealed that we were both right and wrong. We were right about the fact that workers were really unable to help such boys themselves, but we were wrong in believing that a relationship to such boys served no constructive purpose. The constructive purpose just happened to be outside the worker-stake animal relationship.

What really happened when a worker tried repeatedly to counsel, advise, instruct, influence or change a stake animal, was that the other members of the group were doing some important observing and listening, of which we had not, at first, been aware. What we really discovered was an indirect way of communicating with other members of the group. Communications addressed to the stake animal were bouncing off him as if he were a sounding board and

101

ricocheting into the mind and consciousness of the other group members who appeared not to be listening.

We used the term "loud-talking" to explain the technique by which these other minimally involved boys were affected by the worker's attempts to influence the stake animal. The term derives from prison argot and is defined in the *Dictionary of American Underworld Lingo* as follows: "To inform upon a fellow convict by indirection, as to utter such information while within earshot of a guard or a known informer." The object of such loud-talking in prison is, obviously, to get some kind of a favorable response and action from the prison administration, such as getting the other prisoner punished, or at least transferred. It is a technique employed by prisoners to use the machinery of the prison for their own ends while seeming not to appear responsible for the effect their actions have had upon either the prison administration or the person informed upon. The point, however, is that the loud-talker had produced what is, from his point of view, a desirable effect upon a situation he wanted to change. It is a very effective means of communication in that all those within earshot to whom the message is relevant get the full meaning even though they may remain anonymous and their reaction may be delayed.

Similarly, it appeared that some of the youths not immediately involved in direct communication with the worker were able to "get the message" that he was trying to get across to a stake animal or a core member of the group. On the other hand, the stake animal or core member, who was the direct object of the communication, was frequently resistant. He was on the defensive and tried to maintain what he conceived to be his personal integrity. The worker's example, counsel and exhortations were perceived as an attack on the personal qualities of the stake animal by both the stake animal and the others present. The fact that the peripheral members to this intense exchange between the worker and the stake animal saw it this way, however, was precisely what made them receptive to the loud-talking that was going on. The other boys remained open listeners and observers, and were able to accept with greater equanimity that which was being said, insofar as it may have had some application to their own situation. Their defenses were down, they did not feel personally threatened, someone else's troubles were the focus of attention and they were freer to reflect on the logic of the lesson that was being delivered.

The effectiveness of such indirect communication through loud-talking became clear to some of our workers through a number of interesting experiences. Several of our youth groups whose members had not been close to the worker, and had not appeared to be problem-laden on an individual level, began to open up as a result of the worker-stake animal exchanges. Our workers, though pleasantly surprised at the development of better behavior and attitudes, more frequently than not were unable to account for the degree of influence they had upon a group they felt they had been neglecting.

A dramatic example of the loud-talking effect was the case of a boy whom we will call "Jojo." When he first came to our attention, Jojo was a member of a group called the Social Lords. The worker who had picked up this group did not consider them to be de-linquent, although they had a few delinquent members and one all-around problem boy. In terms of status, Jojo was neither a leader nor a core member of the Social Lords, but stood somewhere in the middle ranks. Although reasonably active with the other members of the group, and accepted by them, his relationship to the worker was remote and superficial. The worker viewed Jojo as not seriously delinquent and, while he was not entirely a model of good conduct, he was able to manage his life reasonably well. From almost every point of view he seemed to be one of our typical run-of-the-mill boys.

One day, after about eighteen months of such a peripheral relationship between the worker and Jojo, a remarkable thing happened. Jojo came into one of our outposts in the company of twelve boys who were previously unknown to the worker. He explained that he had organized these boys into a group and that he was their leader. He asked that the worker sponsor this new group just as the worker sponsored the Social Lords. The worker was surprised and bemused for Jojo had neither occupied a leadership position in the Social Lords nor had he displayed the qualities he would require to guide and control the new group. Although skeptical about Jojo's capacity for leadership, the worker agreed to sponsor the group whose continued existence he had every reason to doubt. It should be emphasized that the new group was not a splinter group of either the Social Lords or any other group then being worked with by any of our out-reach workers.

Over the next few weeks the new group took the name "Iroquois" as their own, held a series of meetings, elected their officers and Jojo became president. He not only led the group well but assumed such a conventionally-oriented leadership role that the worker's guidance was hardly necessary. Jojo's means of handling the Iroquois, his personal mannerisms, preachments and methods of social control were almost identical to those employed by the worker in his earlier relationship to the Social Lords. It took a considerable period of time for the worker to get over this almost total assumption of his role on the part of Jojo in relation to the Iroquois. The remarkable feature of this similarity in behavior was that Jojo had seemed to pay little attention to, and have little interest in, the worker's earlier role with the Social Lords. Jojo had, apparently, acquired his learning by indirection, through simply being in the presence of the worker, rather than from any intimate and self-consciously directed interaction between them.

The practical lesson to be learned from these experiences with stake animals and peripheral group members is the usefulness of loud-talking as a self-conscious and deliberate technique for influencing the behavior of others. Rather than abandoning stake animals as a futile enterprise, or feeling guilty about a seeming over-concentration of time, energy and resources on the leadership or core members of a group, workers can take full advantage of the opportunities that these interactional situations present. A perceptive out-reach worker who knows what he is about can, by generalizing his remarks, by raising the level of his voice and by redirecting the relevance of his example and advice, reach a much larger audience and increase his effectiveness as an influence over a group with whom he is working. A station wagon, for example, can be used as a platform and an arena for his role-playing and pronouncements, and the stake animal can serve as a microphone or sounding board for reaching an audience that would otherwise be lost to him. Almost any situation which was formerly reduced to private counseling with a stake animal may be used as an occasion for the rehearsal of a more general application to the problems that others may share, to a lesser degree, with the stake animal. In our search for effective out-reach work techniques we found that loud-talking had a considerable potential. It tended to maximize the worker's effectiveness as an influence with his current clients and, at the same time, seemed to help him to achieve a mass impact over time.

Intervening with the Courts

MOST youthful offenders are not tried in Criminal Court. Special courts have been set up in most jurisdictions for the youthful offender. In Chicago, young offenders usually appear in Juvenile Court if they are under seventeen and in Boys' Court if they are between seventeen and twenty-one. Serious offenses, such as murder, can be tried in Criminal Court but it is not common. Most of the court appearances an out-reach worker makes are in the juvenile courts.

All workers should get themselves a copy of their local Juvenile Court Act and read it and study it until they understand it. If you need help in understanding it, ask the court staff to help you, or talk with lawyers about it. You must thoroughly understand the legal process which applies to youthful offenders.

You must also understand court operations. Some courts have printed up flow charts. If your local court has not done this, make one yourself. A flow chart of the Family Court in Chicago looks like this:

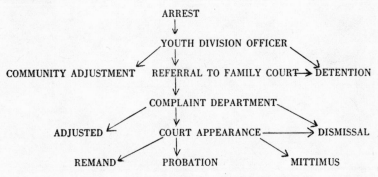

This is, of course, grossly simplified but drawing it out in a chart like this will give you a "feel" for the process.

You should also get, or make up for yourself, an organizational chart of the local juvenile court so you know who everybody is and what they do.

One of the first things you should do after you start working is go to the juvenile court and introduce yourself to everyone. Do not wait until you have a case. Go and meet everyone before you have a case. Write a letter to the Chief Judge or Magistrate requesting a tour of Family Court, explaining your job and why you feel you need to become familiar with the court. It is very important for you to get to know the judges, the people in the Complaint Department, the people in the Probation Department, and the people in the Detention Department. Make yourself familiar with such things as the recreational and educational programs in the Detention Department and even inquire into the quality of the food and the adequacy of bed space. Learn everything you can about the routine and physical conditions in the Detention Department.

Court procedures differ but normally it is the social worker assigned by the court who you will deal with on a case. If you wish to give a statement before the judge in open court, check with the social worker beforehand and ask for his permission. This is a formality but it should be observed. Prepare your statement beforehand. Be brief, concise and to the point. You may make recommendations to the court yourself. A typical statement before a judge might go something like this: "Your Honor, I've known John, the boy before you today, for about six months. He's a member of one of the groups I'm working with as an out-reach worker for the Blank Agency. I'd like to see him given probation, Your Honor. I feel that probation is in the best interests of the boy and of the community. I think John can straighten out, Your Honor, and I hope to work with him and with his family to help him straighten out."

What you say, of course, depends upon the case but you should mention the following in your presentation: How you come to know the boy; how long you have known him; who you are; what you think should be done; and why you think this should be done.

Courts cannot be run to meet the conveniences of the people who appear in them so you may find yourself spending a lot of time just waiting around for your case to come up. Use this time to counsel the youth you are appearing for, and his family. After a while you will learn how to reduce the time you have to spend waiting by doing such things as asking the bailiffs for a time estimate. Bailiffs, incidentally, can be of great help. You should try to get to know them.

The full implications of the recent Supreme Court's "Gault Decision" have not as yet become clear. On the surface, it seems that the decision demands that Juvenile Courts extend due process to the accused, including his full constitutional rights such as defense counsel, trial by jury and so on. Given the volume of cases processed in Juvenile Court, this is next to impossible. Compromises will have to be worked out. It is suggested that workers get a copy of *Gault and the Juvenile Court Revolution,* by James B. George, from the Institute for Continuing Legal Education, Hutchins Hall, Ann Arbor, Michigan. Most Juvenile Court jurisdictions will probably appoint some form of public defenders. The worker is advised to get to know them and work with them.

Relations with the Police

MOST city police departments now have a special Youth Division or Youth Bureau. Dealing with the juvenile offender has become a police work specialty just as Robbery, Homicide, and Traffic are special departments. The great majority of juvenile offenders are arrested by uniformed patrolmen but are soon turned over to Youth Division personnel for processing. The worker, therefore, will have the most frequent and intimate contact with the officers of the Youth Division.

New workers should visit their local police stations as soon as possible after they start working and introduce themselves to the local youth officers. Even if the Youth Officer has had experience in working with out-reach workers before, the new worker should explain his job to him. Different agencies work in different ways and different workers work in different ways. You can't take it for granted that the Youth Officer understands what your job is all about. Make sure he understands what it is you are trying to do in the neighborhood with the youths with whom you are working. Define your job in specific detail to the local Youth Division men and ask for their help. You and your local Youth Division men are both committed to controlling and reducing juvenile delinquency in the neighborhoods you are in. Do not forget that you have the same goals in the long run—the reduction and control of juvenile delinquency. Do not fall into the self-fulfilling prophecy trap and assume that your goals and methods are too divergent for any real cooperation. Assume that your goals are the same and that you can work together. It has been our (CYDP) experience that you can work very profitably with the police, and especially the Youth Division, in the interests of the local youth population.

Chicago was fortunate in having a particularly competent Youth Division as part of its police force. The CYDP worked very closely with such fine officers as Captain Delaney, Lieutenants Bryan and Burke, Sergeants Ford, Davis and Gannon, and Youth Officers Educate, Szwedo, Del Genio and Compasio. There were many others, of course, too numerous to mention, but these men were outstanding.

Workers will find it very helpful to have occasional conferences with the local Youth Division men to discuss neighborhood youth problems. If this is not done formally, it can be done informally. Our workers never made any secret of the fact that we knew the local Youth Division men. The workers would wave to the Youth Division men as they drove by, talked to them openly when they were encountered walking and took phone calls from them in front of groups with whom we were working. Our workers felt friendly toward Youth Division men and they showed it. So far as we can tell this did not affect our relations to youth groups in the least. The amount of hostility felt by inner-city youth for the police is generally high, but this does not mean that inner-city youths do not like humane, competent, police officers. Many police officers are liked and respected by inner-city youth.

A worker's relations with police officers not previously known to him are somewhat more problematical. A worker frequently has to make an "on-the-spot" intervention with patrol officers who are new to the area so the worker doesn't know them and they don't know him.

It helps if you identify yourself and hand the officer a card or some other identification. Say, for example, you came upon two patrolmen trying to get a group you know to move off a corner. You can try something like this: Hand the officer your card and say, "Hello, officer, I'm Joe Doaks. I work for the Blank Youth Agency. I know some of these kids because I work with them. Is there some way I can be of help?" What you say and what you do depends, of course, upon the situation but offer your help. If the officer doesn't want your help, he'll tell you.

Workers are not in the business of helping youth violate the law. At the same time we are not in the business of helping the police act arbitrarily to violate a citizen's civil rights. If you see clear examples of either don't try to turn the street into a courtroom. Cases are heard in courtrooms before judges, not on the streets. If, for example, you come upon an officer using unnecessary force in making an arrest, say something like this: "Look, officer, I'm Joe Doaks and I work for the Blank Agency. I think you don't have to be this rough and I'm willing to say so in court."

This is the extreme, however, for most of the time it suffices simply to let the officers know who you are and the name of your agency. The presence of an observer who might be a witness is usually enough. Never take sides in cases to which you, yourself, were not a witness. The kids you work with are not always right. Neither are the police. Police interventions require the utmost skill and coolness. Do not go off half-cocked. Go off only fully cocked, primed, loaded and well aimed.

Policemen have a very hard job. Do not make their job any harder than it is. In our experience the police will return friendliness and cooperation for friendliness and cooperation.

Getting Drop-Outs Back
in School

EVERY youth who has dropped out of school does not belong back in school. Some are so badly damaged academically that there is little hope for them in the regular school program. The worker has to make a rational assessment about whether a youth he returns to school can stay in school.

The youth's own motivation is extremely important. Does he want to go back? How badly does he want to go back? Can he make it if he does?

How can a worker tell if a youth can make it or not? Past performance is only one of the factors which have to be taken into account. What is critical is not: *did* he do well in the past? What *is* important is: *can* he do well in the future? Try to make an analysis of what the youth was doing that was wrong in the past. You can use the Field Force Analysis Chart. A typical chart might look like this:

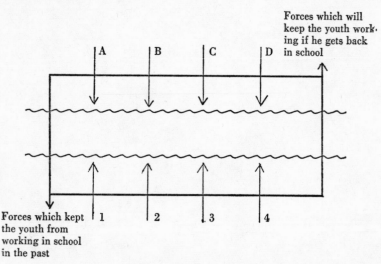

Factors working against the youth include:

1. Dislike of school due to early negative experiences with teachers.
2. History of failure in schoolwork.
3. Inability to see the relevance of the material taught in school.
4. The lure of "freedom" and having one's own money.

Factors working for the youth include:

A. A conviction on the part of the youth that he must get through school or he has "had it."
B. Help from a number of sources, such as tutors, to help overcome the gaps which have developed.
C. Development of a sense of connectedness between school and the world through a counseling relationship.
D. Support for the youth's resolution to complete school from such persons as can be mobilized—worker, parents, peers, etc.

If you "chart out" a youth in this way you can make up a plan for him. Simply getting a youth back to school is not enough. If supports aren't built-in, he will just drop out again. There has to be change in either the youth or the school, or in both. Concentrate on increasing the factors working for the kid and decreasing the factors working against him.

Most schools have counselors. A plan for a youth should be worked out in cooperation with the school counselors. Teachers should be involved in the planning if at all possible.

In dealing with his local schools a worker should be mindful that the schools have procedures and channels. Schools are bureaucratic, hierarchic structures. A worker who is uncomfortable with or resistant to bureaucratic, hierarchic systems is at a disadvantage when it comes to dealing with the local school. The schools must be dealt with as they are. A worker should observe the school's channels, procedures and deference patterns meticulously. Workers should take pains to explain their jobs to all levels of the local school administration. If a worker does not cooperate with the schools, the schools are not likely to cooperate with him.

Tutoring Programs

MOST of our contact population were not doing well in school. A high proportion of them were already drop-outs or were potential drop-outs. Two major surveys undertaken during the years CYDP operated tended to indicate that the schools in our areas were very poor (the Hauser and Havighurst reports). The shoe is frequently put on the wrong foot in the explanations educators offer as to why inner city, lower-class youth do badly in school. The explanation offered is: "Inner city youth do badly in school because they are under-cultured." This simply means that the school culture and the inner city culture do not mesh.

We tried to do what we could to mesh the middle-class culture of most teachers with the lower-class culture of most of our youngsters through the organization of a tutoring program.

What you need to run a tutoring program is:

1. Tutors
2. A place in which to do tutoring
3. Kids who need and are willing to be tutored.

Tutors can be obtained from local colleges and universities. At one time during the CYDP's history we ran a tutoring program using tutors obtained from the honors group of a high school with one of the highest academic ratings in the city of Chicago. With a little effort it is fairly easy to get volunteers for tutorial programs from colleges. The worker must be willing to go to colleges and give talks on the need for tutors, in order to recruit them.

The location you use for tutoring should, of course, be free of distractions. We were able to use a school building after class hours. Churches and recreational agencies during "off" hours can also be used.

114

The kids who need and are willing to be tutored are a little more difficult to come by. You may actually find yourself with more tutors than kids willing to be tutored. Inducements may have to be offered. Recreational features can be built into the tutoring program. Free Cokes, and a social period after the tutoring session can be offered. A "free gym" period can also be used. Recognition in the form of awards for attendance can be considered. The tutoring program will definitely have to be sold in some way. Providing transportation to and from the tutoring center for youngsters is very helpful.

A tutoring program can be maintained only by incessant effort. Absenteeism and tardiness are a problem. It is hard to keep up the pupils' motivation. Workers and tutors conducting a tutoring program will find themselves in a situation where they can offer only long-term rewards and must not resort to punishments. The rewards for the pupil are better grades and learning itself, but with kids whose learning experiences have been negative, the worker must reconcile himself to difficulties. The tutors are rewarded by seeing their pupils learn. They must have a high level of frustration tolerance because it may be a long time before experiences of actually seeing kids learn occur. Running a tutoring program is very hard work. It is also very rewarding work. Helping a kid make it in school is just about the most important thing you can do for him.

The Use of Sports in
Out-Reach Work

TRADITIONAL youth work has placed a heavy emphasis on sports. This emphasis can also be said to characterize out-reach work. We relied very heavily on sports activity in programming for our groups. We tended to view sports as being good for kids' health. It uses up time kids might spend in antisocial activities. It is pro-social. It develops body skills. It is almost a model of the social universe. Everybody had his role to play. Outcome (winning or losing) depends upon teamwork and skill, just as it does in the social universe. It is a kind of microcosm—what is learned in sports activities is transferable to the macrocosm, to the larger social world. In short, sports are good in themselves besides having carry-over values to other contexts. Despite this adult view of sports, when the research team consulted kids as to what important things the worker could do for them, sports was one of the items which rated lowest. If sports are important to inner-city, lower-class youth, it just did not show up in our research. Kids seem to take sports for granted. Indeed, we had workers with little or no interest in sports who worked as effectively with kids as our workers who had degrees in Physical Education. One of our workers had set city track records which still stand, another was a pro basketball player. Most of our workers could and did referee and operate tournaments in basketball and baseball. We even got a number of kids athletic scholarships and sent individuals and teams to all city championship events and tournaments. At times, for brief periods, it seemed that we (CYDP) were one large sports program. Nevertheless, our research indicated that sports were not terribly important to our contact kids. Things which were ranked as more important were that the worker: "gives advice and information," "helps find jobs," and "is a good guy to have around when there is trouble."

Sports should, by all means, be included in any well-rounded program but we feel that it need not have major program emphasis. Inner city youth are much more in need of jobs, and of someone to act as sort of an "ombudsman" for them, than they are of sports. (Note: Ombudsman is a Swedish term for a person who acts as an intermediary between an individual and an institution. The ombudsman acts as a client's representative in the client's dealings with the agencies of the larger society, untangling the bureaucratic red tape in which a person can become ensnarled. Negro youth frequently use the term "my man" for this, while Italian youth frequently use the term "sponsor" for the same thing.)

We held our own tournaments, or involved our teams in tournaments sponsored by other agencies, in basketball, baseball, and volleyball.

We also made extensive use of the following sports activities: 1. swimming; 2. tobogganing; 3. horseshoes; 4. weight-lifting; 5. track and field; 6. go-carting; and 7. skating.

We did not have teams or tournaments for any of these latter activities but it is, of course, entirely possible to do so. We never used boxing in our sports programming but we fed kids into wrestling programs. We did not have any philosophical bias against boxing; we just did not find the kids having much interest in it. We did find a great deal of interest in judo, karate, and akido. Some of our workers knew a little about them but we did not encourage these sports. Judo, karate and akido require enormous discipline and a philosophical orientation which our kids, for the most part, did not have so we left these sports pretty much alone.

If you are going to make extensive use of sports in programming you will have to be prepared for some trouble. Fighting during and after games, by both participants and spectators, is distressingly common. By all means *get good referees*. This cannot be emphasized too strongly. Play on neutral ground whenever you can. Call a game off if things are too hot. Make it an announced policy that "hotheads" are not allowed on the team. The announced policy should be: "You don't play if you don't play fair" and "Hotheads do not play at all."

Jobs

WHEN our research team asked our youngsters what was important to them about the worker, the item ranked third in importance was: "He helps us find jobs." This finding clearly reflects the importance of this aspect of the worker's job. The worker should be a kind of floating employment agency and job counselor.

When the CYDP first started (in 1960) jobs were very hard to get but things improved over the years. The improvement was due to many causes, including the war in Vietnam. There was, however, a concentrated drive by government on all levels to open up employment for youth, especially for high-school drop outs. The single most active agency in the local field of youth employment was the State Employment Service, and we made frequent use of their resources. The private agencies also played their role, holding cooperative Employment Fairs and providing direct service in job finding and employment counseling in many cases.

Workers must make themselves familiar with all of the existing programs and refer youths in need of work to them. However, it will not do, most of the time, to simply tell inner-city youth where the job opportunities are. Workers have to make sure job-seeking youth get to the jobs. A little push is often needed. A worker should consider "walking the kids in" and getting them started. If he doesn't they may never get moving. Workers should take some pains to get to know the staff at the agencies. The worker is advised to "walk" his contacts into the agency and introduce them. The idea is to give the whole thing a kind of personal touch so the youth doesn't feel he's lost in a cold, impersonal, bureaucratic labyrinth. If a worker fails to add these little touches he will find that many of his referrals somehow get "lost" and never get placed.

A worker should prepare kids for the kinds of experiences they're going to have in job finding. At one time the CYDP ran what we called PEP—a Pre-Employment Preparation program. This program was designed by Levert King, a worker in the Henry Horner area. The objective of this program was to educate unemployed youths into knowledgeable employment seekers. We wanted the kids in the program to find themselves jobs worth keeping, and we wanted them to keep the jobs once they found them. These are some of the things which were done:

1) The job seekers were taught to read want ads. It was surprising how few kids knew how to do this in a rational, practical way. They often did not know the meanings of certain terms or abbreviations like shift work, piece work, Blue Cross, per hr., per week.

2) The job seekers were taught the layout of the city, something about the transportation system and how long it was likely to take to get to various employment sites. Job seekers very often didn't know where the job was, or how to get there.

3) All the abbreviations on the check stub were explained— income tax, union dues, insurances, and social security.

4) Attitudes toward work, one's bosses and one's fellow workers were discussed in groups.

5) Speakers from various agencies such as State Employment Service, and personnel managers, spoke to the job seekers.

6) Kids were taught how to fill out application forms.

7) We had kids role play job interviews.

8) There was a graduation ceremony for the job seekers who completed the course.

So far as we can tell this program worked very well. Most kids who started the course finished it. The lesson which was most important was discovering just how much we take for granted about job finding. We do not realize just how complicated the whole process can be for an inexperienced youth. The complications are compounded for inner city, lower-class youth—applications, tests, interviews, physicals and all the rest of the necessary procedures in job finding can lead to panic. They often perform at their very worst in these circumstances and wind up not getting the job. For this reason it is advisable for workers to get to know the people in personnel departments where their contacts often go for jobs. A phone call in the youngster's behalf can often help. This is one of the areas where workers serve as a bridge or ombudsman between the kid and the institutions of the larger society.

The out-reach worker should exploit every existing job resource available. Members of the agency's board should be checked out for jobs. Employment agencies should be looked into for no-fee or low-fee jobs. Trade unions that have apprenticeship programs should be contacted. (Note: It is not enough just to contact employers. You have to establish personal relations with them.) The State Employment Service proved to be our best resource. This was due mostly to Mr. Dan Reid, a very helpful person who was our chief contact with ISES.

Once a youngster has been placed on a job you are not done with him. He will continue to need your support and counseling. You should constantly check those youth who have been placed and be ready to make yourself available for further help and counseling.

Sex

IF you do out-reach work you are going to be working with kids who have come into their full sexual development or who are still in the process. Sex is a preoccupation with them. It is, in fact, almost an obsession. Their vocabulary, especially the incessant, almost obsessional, use of the old, four-letter, Anglo-Saxon term for sexual congress reflects their concern, interest and confusion. Inner city youth, in our experience, are confused about sex and their sex role. Their lack of knowledge of the facts of reproduction, or the specific details of the act, is often startling. You are mistaken if you think lower-class, inner city kids "know all about it." Girls seem to be even more ignorant than the boys about sexual matters. What the boys and girls with whom we worked seemed to know about sex turned out, upon examination, to be a hodgepodge of distortions and plain nonsense.

Workers can, if they wish, close their eyes to the sexual ignorance of their contacts and not deal with it at all. Youth has become fairly accustomed to the fact that most adults are ambivalent about sex and they honor this taboo for the most part. They will not discuss their sex problems with you if you don't want them to do so. Nevertheless, their obsessive preoccupation with sex and their lack of knowledge about it will continue.

If you decide that sex education should be part of your function, you will face many problems. For example, will you have to get parental permission to engage in sex education? If, for example, you want to show movies on sex education, will you have to get agency permission? The same questions apply to movies on venereal disease. Will you have to check with parents before you distribute written materials or recommend books? It's not so much of a problem if a worker is in a "didactic bull session" with his contacts and the topic of sex comes up. The worker can, in this setting, offer his knowledge

121

just as any other participant in the session. If a kid asks a question you give him an answer.

We knew we could be letting ourselves in for trouble if we conducted a semi-formal kind of sex education program but we went ahead and did it anyhow. The trouble we anticipated never did materialize. We showed movies. We passed out literature. We discussed sex in detail in bull sessions and individual counseling sessions. We permitted and encouraged our women volunteers and part-time workers to discuss sex and hygiene with their girls. We did not offer girls courses on the techniques of birth control. We knew we would be laying ourselves open to the charge of promoting promiscuity but it never came. We made no secret of the fact that we provided sex education. We even involved the clergy in it. For a time we had the services of a Jesuit priest from our area whose candidness about sex startled some of our workers. Our good priest minced no words.

We never did go through the formality of obtaining parental permission allowing kids to participate in our informal sex education program. So far as we can tell it wasn't needed. We just assumed that it was part of our job and everybody else seemed to assume the same thing, including the parents.

In our experimental areas the illegitimacy rate was very high but we never saw a girl give her baby up to an agency for adoption. The attitude of many parents seemed to be that it was not a desirable thing but you just accepted it if it happened. We couldn't offer birth control information to girls but we tried to impress on boys the necessity for taking precautions against conception. It probably did not do much good. We don't think we increased the frequency of sex relations in our areas by giving sex education, but we probably didn't decrease it either. The major result seems to have been that our contacts had knowledge where they had nothing but ignorance before. It may be that the only thing which could reduce illegitimacy in areas like ours would be knowledge of birth control techniques on the part of the girls which we felt was something only their parents can give them.

Venereal Disease

VENEREAL disease is said to be increasing among teen-agers. We cannot say on the basis of our experience whether it is or not. We *can* say, however, that we had to deal with it much more often than we liked. Gonorrhea was the most common disease. The vernacular terms for gonorrhea are "clap" and "a dose." Most kids do not know the medical term. We did not observe much overt shame on the part of kids who caught it but one suspects that there was shame and a great deal of fear. It seems fairly safe to assume that kids are not in possession of correct medical information regarding venereal disease. Our workers were very conscious of this and we saw it as one of our legitimate jobs to educate kids regarding vene-real disease. V.D. education was just one of the tasks of public health education in which CYDP workers were constantly involved.

You will probably find, as we did, that the Public Health Depart-ment is more than cooperative. They provided us with literature for distribution, with movies and speakers and most importantly, with treatment. They made treatment quickly and easily obtainable.

In getting kids to go in for treatment you may encounter strong resistance. All kinds of stupid myths about treatment are in circula-tion. The Health Department is very often seen as punitive and pry-ing; kids who have V.D. are very reluctant to give their names to the Health Department and to tell where they contracted their V.D. The Health Department tries as hard as it can to locate the source of contamination but in our experience it doesn't use coercion in any way. We have urged kids to cooperate with them in locating the source so the source can be treated, but we were not always able to convince them to do so. In one case where a number of boys all had been contaminated by one girl we were able to use neighborhood pressure to get her treated privately. We contacted a neighbor of the girl who brought pressure on her brother to get her treated.

Very often kids will tell you that they never saw the girl before and had only one contact with her. This is often the case but it is often not the case. Press very hard on boys to find out who gave them the dose. Often if they don't know, they can find out, or "suddenly" they will "remember" and be able to tell you so you can tell the Health Department. Sometimes kids do not want to tell the Health Department themselves, but they'll tell you so *you* can tell them.

Let it be known in the area you're working in that you are a person who can get treatment for V.D. Define yourself as a Public Health Resource. Soon after you start working in an area visit your local public health facility and establish relations with the people who have charge of V.D. control. We were able to make arrangements with them to "walk a boy in" by just calling on the phone beforehand. We found that it was important to "take" boys in for treatment. They need reassurance and they may keep putting it off unless you literally take them by the hand and lead them in. Once you become known as a person who will "fix it up" for kids with V.D., you'll get plenty of requests for help.

Camping Programs

THE camps which are run by most youth-serving agencies are not designed for teenagers. The age of the average camper in most agency camp programs is about twelve or thirteen. The median age of the boys reached by the CYDP program was about 15.6. There are a few special camp programs throughout the country which are designed for boys in our age group but they were not available to us. So, in effect, we had to work out our own camp program.

We had access to a number of camps on a special short-term basis. We could not bring our groups to the different camps we used while their regular program was in operation because there was simply no room. Regular camp programs in our area operate during the summer months so the camp program we worked out was almost invariably "off season." That is, we camped in fall, winter and spring.

We saw camping as providing an opportunity for developing the relationship between the worker and his group. We deliberately kept the groups small.

We saw camp as a setting in which the provocations and lures of city-street life would be minimized, providing the worker with an opportunity to come to know his groups better. At camp a worker could be with his groups for thirty-six or forty-eight hours at a stretch. It might take months to put this many hours in with a group in the city.

A typical winter week end camp program for CYDP workers and their groups would go something like this:

Friday

8:00 P.M.   Arrival. Assign bunks and store gear. Meeting to orient camp set-up.

8:40 P.M.   Snack

Friday

9:15 P.M.   Meeting to discuss work assignments, cleanup and maintenance.

9:30 P.M.   Activities: short hike if possible or any other physical activity that's available.

10:30 P.M.   Bedtime: Note: in our experience very little sleeping is done the first night out.

Saturday

7:00 A.M.   Rise

7:20 A.M.   Breakfast

8:15 A.M.   Cleanup

9:30 A.M.   Tour of camp facilities

10:30 A.M.   Activities (whatever is available)

12:00 P.M.   Lunch

1:30 P.M.   Group discussion

2:30 P.M.   Activities

5:00 P.M.   Supper

6:30 P.M.   Activities

9:30 P.M.   Group discussion and snack (Note: we frequently showed movies at this time.)

10:30 P.M.   Bed

Sunday

7:00 A.M.   Rise

7:20 A.M.   Breakfast

8:15 A.M.   Cleanup

10:00 A.M.   Depart for home

During the activities periods we had sledding, hikes, team sports, rides in the country, ice-pond activities like skating, and so on.

One of the camps we used was an old estate which had been donated to a youth-serving agency. The setting was really not much like a camp so we did not try to make it seem like one. We treated trips to this converted estate like a "week end in the country" rather than a camping trip. We even had girls' groups come up for a day to this location.

Camping definitely provides an opportunity for a worker to come to know his groups better. We have found that it is best to keep the stay at camp short and the groups small. A worker should not try to supervise more than eight youths at camp. The schedule should be kept very tight. Do not leave a lot of free time. Make it very clear to the group before you go to camp that everybody is going to have to do some work and even make work assignments before you leave the city.

Orient the regular camp staff such as cooks and caretakers to your groups. If you don't do this then you can expect trouble.

The trip to and from camp is an important activity in itself and should be exploited for its didactic bull session possibilities.

The Armed Services

IT is part of American "folk wisdom" that what many delinquent youth need is to have some backbone put into them. It is widely believed that the control and discipline to which one is subjected in the armed services is "good" for irresponsible, unruly youths. Some cynics have referred to military schools as "reform schools for rich kids." In years gone by some "reform schools" were in fact para-military in their operations and ex-military men could often find jobs as administrators of correctional institutions. It is axiomatic in our society that the military has a beneficial effect on young men. It "straightens them out."

So far as we can tell there is more than a little truth in these ideas. Many youths do drop their delinquent ways in the services. They may drop their old habits and pick up some equally bad ones, but all in all a very high proportion of the delinquents we have known do "settle down" while in the service. Cynics will say they would have settled down anyway because they are getting older and the services just "put a guy on ice" for a while. The devil finds work for idle hands and so does the military. The work that the services find for one to do varies from the meaningless to the terribly significant, but it is always work and one does get paid for it. There is even the remote possibility that one can learn something that will be useful in civilian life.

Our workers often urged and helped youths get into the services.

A great many of the youths we knew could not pass the mental examinations so we obtained Preparation Manuals from our local recruiters and coached many of the youths whom we knew so that they could pass the exams. Many had trouble getting into the service because they had "records."

If the boy was on parole or probation, consent had to be obtained from the court to let him join the service. This of course was contingent upon the recruiting officer indicating to the court that the service would accept the boy.

What was involved for the most part was a "selling job" on the part of the worker to the recruiting officer. The recruiting officer had to be persuaded to "take a chance" on the boy. This involved some risk on the part of the recruiter, but they were usually willing to take it. One of the greatest selling points was the probabilities of a youth's making it. The worker would say something like this to the recruiter: "In the last year I've gotten ten guys in the service who were in the same situation as this kid. Only one kid has so far gotten a D.D.; all the other guys are doing fine."

When the recruiter has some idea of just how much risk is involved for him he can make his own decision.

Most of the youths we helped get into the service worked out all right. A few did get Bad Conduct and Undesirable discharges, but the overwhelming majority did very well.

The service is definitely not a solution to all youth problems. Workers are best advised not to try to talk youths into it but only to help them if they have an interest.

Working with Girls' Groups

IN the original design of the CYDP action program girls were not included in the designated target population. We knew of course that we would have to do indirect work with girls, *i.e.*, through volunteers and community organizations, but we found ourselves obliged throughout the history of the CYDP to do some direct work with girls' groups. Normally the total number of girls we had involved in program groups did not exceed fifty. This was a ratio of about one girl to every six boys in our program groups. We worked with our girls' groups through female volunteers and part-time female workers. The girls, however, persisted in regarding one or another of the male workers as "their workers." Even when it became clear to them that the male worker would simply turn all requests for service and programming back to their female worker, the girls persisted in maintaining an identity with their initially contacted male worker. So much so, in fact, that we must say that the male staff member never really severed his relationship with a girls' group but continued to play a part in the groups' relationship to the CYDP.

Initially our attempt was to connect our girl's groups to other agencies, but there was so little in the way of program for girls in our area that we had to set up program for girls ourselves. We were able to get female volunteers from our community organization efforts but we had to have the volunteers work out of our facilities, such as the Outpost. We did make it a rule, however, that girls could only come to our facilities on a prearranged basis. They could not "drop in" as boys could. We did not permit girls to "hang around" at the Outpost.

Many superficial observers of inner city youth get the impression that inner city girls are sexually loose and do not care about their reputations. This is not true. Most inner city girls are not sexually

130

loose and care very much about their reputations. There is more overt sexuality because there is less privacy. Inner city youth do not live in a world in which it is easy to hide things. Their speech and their dancing have a high sexual content but this is not necessarily true of their private behavior. Privately they are probably more confused and scared about sex than middle-class suburban youth.

It is true that young inner city girls more frequently get pregnant than their suburban sisters but this is not due to a general moral laxity on their part. A generalization which may be made on the basis of some of the sociological literature on unwed motherhood is that the girl who becomes an unwed mother has not engaged in sexual behavior for its own sake but rather in the hope that the relationship would or could develop into something *more* than a sexual relationship. In our society it is the male who engages in sex as a form of self-aggrandizement. Male status is enhanced by sexual promiscuity while female status declines as a consequence of sexual promiscuity.

We wanted to help those girls whom we had in our program groups become less likely to become "unwed mothers." We reasoned that they were likely to become unwed mothers because they tended to have very low self-esteem. Jokingly the goal in programming for girls was once stated as: "We've got to make them marriageable." We reasoned that girls who had the long-range goal of marriage, home and family, and the skills which would permit them to perform in the role of married women, would be less likely to get pregnant. We found that girls were very much interested in what we might call the "social aspects" of a woman's role in American society. The girls were interested in what we must call for want of a better term "display." They were very interested in clothes and makeup classes, for example. Etiquette and charm classes attracted them strongly. Our volunteers taught these classes and did things like just sitting around and discussing the contents of women's magazines, even the advertisements. One popular program activity was "going downtown shopping." On these trips the volunteers taught the girls the layout of stores, what stores were in what price ranges, quality of merchandise and so on. Downtown shopping was a completely new world to many of the girls. Talking to clerks and eating in restaurants were often so threatening that they simply couldn't do it.

Girls were, if anything, even more avid for just "riding around" than boys.

Much of the impetus for the more formal and conventional types of program activities came from girls. They wanted "dress-up" socials, picnics, beach parties and sleigh rides in winter. They were frequently overambitious and wanted to take on more than they could do. We taught baton-twirling to our girls' groups and helped them make up singing groups. They put on talent shows and held teas for their parents. The girls seemed to like what the boys called "square" activities.

A curious thing happened: Our boys' groups and our girls' frequently grew apart. It does seem to be true that girls mature socially faster than boys; at any rate the boys and girls we had in program frequently drifted out of each others' spheres of interest so that it was very easy to program for them separately. The girls' groups, most of the time, ceased being adjuncts to boys' groups and had their own existence. We did not intend for this to happen but we did not try to stop it.

It is hard to evaluate the effectiveness of our work with girls. Since they were not initially part of the target population no research was done on them by our research component. We do have the impression, however, that very few of the girls we had in program groups got into trouble with the law. Very few were ever arrested.

Drinking Behavior

DRINKING by teenagers takes place in a variety of settings and functions to fulfill a number of needs and goals for the drinkers. It is very important for anyone who has to deal with drinking by teenagers to have some feel for the goals teenagers have in drinking.

Some Possible Goals Teenagers Have

1. Drinking is adult behavior. I'm like an adult when I drink and that's what I want to be like.
2. Drinking is forbidden. Anything forbidden must be fun and I want some fun.
3. Everybody will call me "square" and rank me if I hold back from drinking when everybody else is.
4. They say drinking helps you forget your troubles and have a good time and I want to forget my troubles and have a good time.
5. Why not drink? Everybody's doing it. In this neighborhood all kids drink and always have.
6. Drinking and getting drunk is one very clear way to tell the people who make the rules that you don't give a rap for their goddamn rules.
7. Drinking makes me less shy and uncomfortable at social events. I drink to reduce my tensions.
8. You can get away with a lot if people think you're drunk and don't know any better.

These are just some of the goals kids have for drinking but it's probably safe to say that for teenagers drinking is never an end in itself.

Drinking seems to be very much wrapped up in how a kid feels about himself. It's our impression that kids who have high regard for themselves and who feel that their peer groups hold them in high regard tend to drink minimally or not at all. Kids who do not hold themselves in high regard and who feel that their groups do not hold them in high regard seem to drink more. Of course there is a certain amount of "experimental drinking" in which most kids seem to get involved at one time or another. There is also a lot of "show drinking" in which kids sometimes convince even themselves that they are drinking when they are really not. Drunkenness can be staged like anything else for the effect it produces on the audience and can be an indirect plea for attention, care and help. Drinking is an ideal attention-getting device for those kids (and there are many) who feel that you have to be "bad" to get any attention at all.

Handling drunk kids in a public setting is one of the stickiest jobs a worker comes up against. We have found it helpful to use role playing in training workers for this kind of job. One worker simply takes the role of a drunk kid and acts as nasty, obstreperous, and "clowny" as he possibly can. It's another worker's role to settle him down and take care of him. This kind of role play should be gone over and over again in training workers until they have an extensive variety of techniques in their repertoire. The object is to develop ease and faciilty. There is no one right way to do it. The goal is to make the worker sure of himself and his ability. Once a kid is drunk it takes a long time to sober him up—very often, more time than the worker has. What has to be worked on is the kid's attitude toward the fact of his own drunkenness. He has to be talked into "playing it cool" until he's sober. This involves getting out of public sight until he's sober and stopping his drinking. As has been pointed out, this is very hard to do. A worker can expect to encounter failures in these efforts.

Before any program activity which you hold, make a kind of "contract" with the kids who are likely to be there. The contract is this: anyone who drinks or acts like he's been drinking cannot take part in the activity. You have the right to confiscate bottles. The group must assist you in enforcing the no-drinking rule.

The Use of Volunteers

THE use of volunteers in out-reach programs has not been extensive. It is very hard to be a part-time out-reach worker. We (CYDP) never did use male part-time workers but we did make some use of volunteers who supervised activities of those groups who met regularly in the Outpost and the Chicago Boys Clubs' buildings. We were able, in a number of cases, to transfer groups over to a volunteer who saw the group only once or twice a week and for special events, particularly in the case of girls' groups.

Most of our volunteers were people who lived in the areas where we worked. We had a number of mothers, some of whom had children in groups we worked with, who we could always rely on as chaperones and for additional supervision on trips and tours. We made arduous attempts to get men from the area to serve as volunteers but we had little success in doing this. Some of our women were with us almost the full length of the Project history (six years).

Out-reach work defies "routinization" and this was one of the major problems in working with volunteers. For example, we could not say to a volunteer, "Okay, you be here from now on at 7:30 P.M. every Tuesday and a group will be here to meet with you." It just isn't this easy. Volunteers who are strangers to the neighborhood are at a considerable disadvantage. If their groups don't show, for example, they don't know where to go looking for them. And no matter how interested and good-willed they are much of the behavior of their groups baffles and overwhelms them. Signs of change, for example, are few and far between. It's very hard for a volunteer to get some idea of how he or she is doing. The volunteer gets caught in what Hayakawa calls the IFD syndrome. They come in with all kinds of illusions about how they are going to help "these kids." Their best efforts don't pay off. Frustration follows and then Disillusion which leads to more Illusion, Frustration, Disillusion.

A volunteer in an out-reach program has to be given considerable preparation for the work. We usually began preparing the volunteers with a long "hang around" period, lasting as long as two months. During this period the volunteers stayed very close to the worker two or three nights a week for three or four hours. Frequent discussions were held with volunteers to help them develop and elaborate their perceptions. Volunteers should have regular supervisory conferences. The volunteers were gradually placed in situations in which they interacted by themselves with the groups to see how they made out. For example, a volunteer would be asked to drive a group of youths to the beach, let them off there and pick them up later.

We always had an explicit verbal contract with the volunteers. The volunteer had no obligation to take a group. If it didn't work out we both could just say, "Sorry, and thanks for your time."

Our most successful volunteers were those who we could tie to groups who had regular meetings. We were not interested in obtaining volunteers who were entranced with the lure of street life and who were looking for "kicks." There are such people around and you have to be wary of them. There is a lot of work involved in incorporating volunteers into an out-reach program but, all in all, it's worth it.

Weapons

IT is very easy to set a weapons policy. It is very hard to stick to it. In most states and jurisdictions it is against the law for a minor or adult to carry a concealed, lethal weapon.

A person who has knowledge that someone else is carrying a weapon and who fails to report it, can be tried as a party to a crime or as an accessory to a crime. It can be either a misdemeanor or a felony depending on the situation and the jurisdiction.

The worker who knows a kid has a weapon is under considerable pressure to either report it or have the kid get rid of it. The worker is in a terrific "double bind." If he reports it, he will probably destroy his relationship with the kid and he may get himself tabbed a "fink," destroying the possibility that he can continue working. If he doesn't report it, he's in danger of arrest and people, including the carrier, are in danger.

A worker will not get anywhere in handling the problem of weapons-carrying unless he has some understanding as to why kids carry weapons in the first place.

Kids say they carry weapons "for protection." This answer shouldn't be simply dismissed. A kid conceivably can have a legitimate need for protection. The plea, "I need it to protect myself" can be based on a very realistic appreciation of a particular kid's situation. Try putting yourself in the kid's situation. If you were he would you carry a weapon? The best way to find out why a kid packs a weapon is to ask him. Ask him and listen credulously to what he says. Don't start attacking or arguing against it before you know why.

Weapons for most kids are not purely utilitarian articles. Weapons are insignia, badges of identity, symbols of something else. A kid's whole feeling of masculinity, for example, can be wrapped up in his knife or his gun. A knife or a gun can be for a kid a kind of magical

137

proof of potency. He would feel naked, alone and helpless without it. It's often his "security." It may seem odd but a weapon can function for a kid just like a security blanket.

A gun can cost $50.00, a knife $5.00. Enormous effort and risk have frequently gone into getting weapons. When you ask a kid to give up a weapon, have some appreciation of what it is you're asking him to do. You're asking him very often to give up money, effort, and even a piece of himself.

The trick is this: You've got to reduce the threat that being unarmed represents to the kid. The threat is not just physical harm. The threat is to the kid's self-esteem and self-concept. The weapon may be like a magical charm which literally keeps the kid's self-image intact.

One of the first things you want to find out about any weapon is: "Who owns it?" Very often a weapon a kid has in his possession does not belong to him. It may be a friend's, or a relative's. The ownership of the weapon may be a factor you can play on to make the kid get rid of it.

We have found that there is no use "beating about the bush" regarding weapons. You should tell kids quite frankly that you're against weapons-carrying and you don't want to be around kids who carry them. You should also make it clear that you will not take a weapon and return it later. Once you've been given a weapon, you destroy it. Knives you can destroy by placing them open on a gutter in the street and stepping on them. Drop the two pieces in the sewer. Guns should have their hammers and/or pins removed or be dismantled entirely. If you've got a convenient body of water, drop it in. Some workers in some agencies turn weapons over to the police who dispose of them through their channels. This usually means the weapon will be "checked out." You should be aware of the possible implications of this "checking-out." Ask the police what's involved if you're going to give them weapons for disposal.

This whole problem admits of no easy solution. Nations have not worked out the problem of disarmament, neither have out-reach workers.

Training Out-Reach Workers

MOST out-reach workers learned their trade by doing it. Frequently there has been a kind of master-apprentice training procedure where an inexperienced worker "hangs around" with an experienced worker and learns his trade by participant observation. There is really nothing much in the way of systematic training. We hope, of course, that this book will be useful and we have included a list of suggested publications which we think a novice worker should read. All that we can include here really are some suggestions for training workers.

Workers should make a very formal survey of the area they are going to work in. It is not enough to simply read the census data. One way of doing this is to have the novice worker do a survey himself. A survey instrument should be designed for this. It's not enough to tell a worker just to "go out and take a look at the area." A survey will force a worker to organize his perceptions. In designing the survey, the "unit of analysis" should be decided upon. Most cities are composed of blocks and the block is probably the most useful unit of analysis.

Once the unit of analysis is decided upon sheets should be printed up, one for each unit. The sheets should contain blanks which have to be filled in with the correct information regarding such things as: Type of block—Residential, Commercial, Industrial, etc.; Number of people visible at what time of day; What kinds of people; Race; Age; Sex; Condition of buildings—Sound, Deteriorated; Dilapidated; Type of building units—House, Apartments, Other; Percentage of each. Schools, churches, social agencies and other institutions should be noted.

The form of the survey should, of course, be determined by the specific agency a worker is going to work for. The above suggestions are only general.

Novice workers should have a period in which they are required to go around introducing themselves to the people in the area who are concerned with youth—teachers, clergy, social agency staffs, police, and anyone else interested in youth and youth problems.

Novice workers should get a thorough grounding in the local laws which pertain to juveniles and learn the local court structure and operations. Visits should also be made to all the institutions which hold youths in custody.

If there are already workers on the job a kind of quasi-Master-Apprentice relationship should be set up. Novices should be given a period in which they are participant observers with more experienced workers.

Role playing can be used extensively in the training of workers. Role plays such as handling drunken kids, for example, should be played out. Role playing can be done by two people or a group with everyone switching roles around. Role playing is just about the only way to prepare a novice worker for the kinds of situations he's going to encounter and it should be intensively used in training.

Talks and lectures are of course useful.

Contact, formal and informal, with more experienced workers seems to be one of the most productive methods of training. There seems to be something about association with experienced workers in itself which gives the novice confidence.

Some False Public Images of
Gangs and Gang Delinquency

IMAGE: Most gangs are made up of "toughs" who are constantly looking for a fight or for something to steal.

In our experience this is not true. Most of the activity of so-called teenage gang groups is quite conventional. Few delinquents are delinquent all of the time. Even the wicked do rest. If gangs were as bad, in fact, as they are often depicted in movies, for example, most gang members would become professional full-time criminals when they get older. This, of course, they do not do. Most gang members will become fathers and husbands and holders of steady jobs who will be indistinguishable from their neighbors. No more than ten per cent of gang members will eventually become professional criminals.

Gang members seem above all to be concerned with not having themselves defined as childish and harmless so their postures, gestures, language and so on have a kind of masculine excessiveness which threatens many people.

Are gang members anxious to convey to the public the idea that they are in fact dangerous?

It seems as though they are and for good reason. If they appear vulnerable they are open to attack. It is not safe to appear vulnerable. They are caught in a vicious circle. They must appear tough or they will be attacked. Their tough appearance mobilizes a reaction on the part of others to their appearance so their tough appearance is for them warranted.

They must appear tough or they will be attacked, and because they *do* appear tough they *are* attacked or at the very least avoided, which also corroborates their impression that they must appear tough.

Toughness for people is very much like it is for some animals.

It's mostly display. Those displaying toughness very often don't want to fight and will avoid it if they can but they must appear ready or else they will have to fight. It's a kind of selective blindness. They are creating the very situation they are trying to avoid.

A worker is not, however, well advised to treat the apparent "toughness" of his groups lightly until he knows them very well. Conversely, a worker is not well advised to take it too seriously. Most of it is bluster but treating it as mere bluster will turn it into something real. Always allow gang members to save face. Gang members are often as sensitive to loss of face as a bunch of Japanese samurai.

Image: The leader of a gang is usually the toughest, strongest kid in the group who has his position because he can or has beaten every member of the group in a fight.

This is not true in our experience. Gang leaders tend to be natural leaders. Most leaders of gangs do not spend a lot of time fighting with their own groups, or with other groups, for that matter. The natural leader usually possesses an acute awareness of the needs, interests and motivations of his own group. He has therefore an acute perception of "what will work." "Doc" of Whyte's *Street Corner Society* exemplifies the natural leader who knows what group consensus is without having to test for it. The natural leader can predict accurately what group consensus will be. He does not necessarily determine it. He can, however, predict it and in effect can "choose" to do what the group wants to do anyway. Our workers almost invariably got along very well with the leaders of the groups we worked with and they helped the workers lead the groups in a pro-social direction.

Image: Drug use by gang members is very high.

Not in our experience. In five years of experience with hundreds of gang members we have known only two or three boys who became regular "hard" drug users. Even marijuana use was not common. In our experience kids do not have easy access to drugs and seem to be afraid of them even when they are available. Drinking is much more of a problem. The drug user was held in contempt in the areas where we worked and kids avoided obtaining the "junkie" identification. Those few who used drugs did not do so openly. Drug users were on the bottom of the local status system.

The Chicago Police Department Youth Division does not pick up more than fifty juveniles a year for drug use.

Image: The girls who associate with boys' groups are sexually promiscuous to a high degree.

This was not borne out in our experience. There may, in fact, be more sexual behavior by suburban girls than there was by the girls who associated with our groups. There were, in the areas where our project went forward, a few girls who "put out for anybody" but they were few and far between. Most of the girls so far as we could tell did not have any sex relations at all. The girls who got pregnant usually got that way from boys with whom they thought they had an "understanding." Usually they had misinterpreted the boys' intentions and wound up knocked-up.

Heavy petting and sexy dancing frequently went on at parties but it did not normally lead to consummation in the sex act.

Image: Gangs are well organized, coordinated groups with stability, continuity and a complex division of labor. They have large membership, well articulated goals, and all of the other characteristics of an efficient, effective organization.

Normally exactly the opposite is the case. Few human organizations are very efficient to begin with and gangs are definitely among the least efficient of human organizations. Gang members, of course, frequently try to convey the impression that their groups are large, efficient, and powerful. This is usually pure fantasy.

Leon Jansyn, of the University of Southern Illinois, distinguishes three degrees of gang membership: (1) Core group membership; (2) conventional membership; and (3) fantasy membership. Jansyn found, in studying one of the most infamous groups in Chicago, that membership, as estimated by the members of the group, differed over time. Size of membership as estimated by the group seemed to be a function of what was going on at the time and who was asking the question. During times of quiet and involvement in conventional activities, estimates of membership were low. During periods of stress and threat, estimates of group size reached fantastic numbers. Many youths were willing to claim membership on the most tenuous grounds; just having once attended a dance held by the group seemed to enable many youths to claim membership. During times of stress the core group, of course, might even validate the claim but definitely not in normal circumstances.

Gang groups very obviously enjoy the attentions they get from the mass media and have learned what "image" the media wants. Some gang groups can create an image with all the skill of a public-relations man. Anyone who has an image of gang groups derived from newspapers has a false image; even the so-called "in-depth" articles and series are not much good. In fact, they are downright misleading.

A Week in the Life of an
Out-Reach Worker

INTRODUCTION: The question: What does an out-reach worker do? can be answered in a variety of ways. Before the question is answered in the abstract, in terms of "process" and "function," it may be well to reproduce that experience in as nearly a concrete form as the nature of the written word permits.

Reproduced below are the edited copies of the Daily Activity Reports of EW-19, a worker for the Chicago Youth Development Project of the Chicago Boys Clubs. His reports cover the Period December 6-11, 1965, and they have been edited only with respect to the confidentiality of human relations: the names of individual boys and the names of the street groups to which they belong have been transliterated into appropriate pseudonyms. Everything else except exact addresses has been retained.

At the time these reports were written, EW-19 had been employed as a worker for just nine months. He is twenty-three years old, white, single, and has a B.A. in Philosophy from a small, Midwestern, religiously-oriented college. He is working on Chicago's near-south-west side in the area surrounding the Oldtown Chicago Boys Club (corner Taylor and Racine Streets). The population in that area is fifty per cent Italian, twenty-five per cent Negro and twenty-five per cent Mexican and Puerto Rican. Most of EW-19's clients are either Negroes or Mexicans. He is considered a dedicated and competent worker and this week of work is fairly representative of his round of activities.

*　　*　　*

MONDAY

1:30 P.M.   I arrived at OBC [Oldtown Chicago Boys Club]. George Wilson [15], and J. T. Carter [14] were standing in front of OBC. Both said they were dismissed early from school, but Carter has been truant from Montefiore [the Board of Education's disciplinary or "adjustment" school] several days in the last two weeks.

2:30 P.M.   Ron Wolsfeld, CRC, [the CYDP community organizer in the OBC area] and I patrolled the Jackson School area. No youths were loitering in Sheridan Park as was the case last week. There were no incidents. [There had been some trouble near this public school and public park recently.]

3:00 P.M.   We returned to OBC. Tommy "Bug" Rodriquez [15] was standing in front of OBC. In response to my question, he said he didn't go to school today. With concern, I advised that he go if he doesn't want to end up in Parental School [the Board of Education's residential disciplinary school] or Montefiore.

3:30 P.M.   I called the Halsted Progress Center and they informed me that they are still processing the applications for employment or other help for Carl [17] and Mark [15] Perkins. I then called Allan Booker [17] who said he is still interested in putting on a play. He told me that about three of the "Town Apostles" [15-19] are now working at Memorial Hospital nights. I talked to him about the apprenticeship programs Paul Mallory [of Transo Envelope Co.] spoke to me about and he is interested. Melvin Harris [21] came to OBC and asked if by any chance I had a possible job for him. He had been working at Alden's but was released as the result of an intense argument with another employee. I called Dan Reid [Illinois State Employment Services-Counselor] and made an appointment with him for Melvin Harris tomorrow morning.

4:00 P.M.   John Ford [15] came to OBC looking for T. Rodriquez. I told him that I was very concerned about T. Rodriquez's recent truancy: "If you have a chance, hit on him about school—I don't want to see him screw himself up simply because he doesn't feel like going."

4:30 P.M.   I called Paul Mallory, who has three apprenticeship programs, to find out if he will hire youth who have records. At present, he is also getting referrals from IYC [the Illinois Youth Commission] and is especially interested in dropouts. The three programs: 1) machine adjuster, 2) die cutter, and 3) printer, are approved by the U.S. Dept. of Labor.

5:00 P.M. I attended the OBC Program Staff meeting for the purpose of planning OBC Xmas activities. CYDP-OBC staff will be responsible, with Burnett Murrell [OBC staff] having the main responsibility for a teen dance (12/23/65).

6:00 P.M. I drove 8 boys [11-14] to the Duncan YMCA for swimming.

6:30 P.M. I went home. I was due some compensatory time off.

* * *

TUESDAY

1:30 P.M. I arrived at OBC.

2:00 P.M. Ezra Smith, EW, [the other CYDP street club worker in the OBC area] and I drove to the HHBC-OP [Henry Horner Chicago Boys Club Outpost]. All the CYDP staff met with Prof. Saul Berstein from Boston University School of Social Work regarding some research he is doing. We discussed such matters as youth work and potential riot situations, our reactions to the Anti-Poverty Program, and recommendations we would make regarding education and other services for so-called hard-to-reach youth.

5:00 P.M. We returned to OBC. Patti Kemper [an OBC staff member in charge of the Guidance in Education and Employment Project] told me that Mr. Burton "Bud" Shaffer [former OBC Board Member] is looking for a shipping clerk to work in the Merchandise Mart. I told her about Melvin Harris who had asked me about a job yesterday. I had referred him to Dan Reid today. When I called Harris, he told me he had received two job offers today, but is interested in learning more about the shipping clerk position. He will come to OBC this evening to talk to P. Kemper. I then called Fred Martin's [17] mother to ask if she knew when her son was to be in court for allegedly stealing a tape recorder from the HPC [Halsted Progress Center]. She hadn't received any notification. I suggested that she encourage her son to go to HPC tomorrow and talk to Obern Simons [former Asst. Dir. of OBC and now on the staff of the HPC]. Martin is on the NYC [Neighborhood Youth Corps] payroll at the HPC.

6:00 P.M. Jimmy McMullan [17] came to OBC and, with some embarrassment, told me that his wife told him that he hasn't "satisfied" her sexually. He said that both of them were virgins at the time of meeting each other. He was very concerned and is considering seeing a doctor, believing that he might be impotent. We then talked about various aspects of sexual intercourse and it became apparent that he was unaware of pertinent facts.

7:30 P.M. I left the area for home. I was due some compensatory time off.

Comment: It was gratifying to me that McMullan felt free to share such a personal concern with me. I have spent considerable time with him, possibly too much time to be devoted to one youth, but I am reminded of the Stake-Animal concept. Some effeminate characteristics in him were evident to me during the first few months of our relationship, which I felt were due to a tremendously possessive mother and the absence of a father or other respected male figure in his home.

McMullan is an influential member of an unnamed group of approximately 6 boys [15-18] most of whom have records of police adjustments. At least two are highly respected for their street fighting ability and one is frequently truant and has been involved in more serious delinquent behavior, at times with other members of this group. Not long after I met McMullan and other members of this group, one of them, Isaac "Gene" Jackson [16], expressed the concern that he was afraid McMullan would become a "fag."

* * *

WEDNESDAY

1:00 P.M. I arrived at OBC.

1:30 P.M. Melvin Harris called to tell me he is going to the Merchandise Mart to apply for the shipping clerk job made available by Mr. Shaffer.

2:00 P.M. I drove to the American Friends Service Committee Project House, 35XX W. Jackson Blvd.

2:30 P.M. I made some home visits on police referrals: No one was home at the Rizzo residence, 15XX W. Polk St. At the home of Felix Gonzalez [14], 14XX W. Fillmore St., I talked to Mrs. Gonzalez and Pete Gonzalez [16]. F. Gonzalez has been chronically truant all year. At 14XX W. Fillmore St., I talked to Mr. and Mrs. Ramos about their son, David [4], who was the victim of a sexual advance by Jack "Loco" Sanchez [16], who, apparently, has a previous record of sex offenses. The parents are interested in the OBC program and plan to send their four oldest sons [8-12] to OBC for membership. Mr. Ramos may prove to be an effective volunteer for such activities as weekend camping trips.

4:30 P.M. I returned to OBC. Peter Miscinski [an OBC staff member who tutors in the GEEP project] told me that Jesse Rivera [14], who has been going through an acting-out period, will be at OBC this evening for a meeting regarding a scholarship for which he and two other "Spanish Squires" [14-16] are being considered. Earl Doty, AD, [the CYDP community organization Supervisor] and the OBC-CYDP staff informally discussed the situation at Crane High School and the activities of the RIO [Riis School Improvement Organization] and MSF [Mile Square Federation].

5:30 P.M. I wrote yesterday's Daily Activity Report.

6:00 P.M. I called Mrs. Booker and asked her to tell Allan Booker [17] to be at OBC at 3:00 P.M. tomorrow. Transo Envelope Co. will consider him for one of their apprentice programs at 35XX N. Kimball Ave. When I called Mrs. Martin, she informed me that she still has received no word concerning her son's court date. I then called Maxwell and Monroe police stations, but was unable to learn anything. I again called Mrs. Martin to tell her son that Obern Simons [HPC] will be expecting him at 10:00 A.M. tomorrow morning. I told her that O. Simons and I had discussed the possibility of getting F. Martin back into the Job Corps. He had been at a Job Corps Center in Texas for about 6 months, but was released because of excessive AWOL's.

7:00 P.M. I completed yesterday's Daily Activity Report.

8:00 P.M. Ezra Smith, EW, and I drove to Duncan-Maxwell YMCA to talk to the "Jive Town" boys who hang out there concerning the tension at Jackson Branch of Crane High School. We talked to two separate groups of 15 boys each [13-17]. E. Smith did most of the talking, emphasizing that a "race riot" certainly solves no problems and referring to Dr. Martin L. King's efforts through non-violence. Since they continued to sound belligerent, Smith cautioned them if need be, rely on "your God-given hands," not weapons. One of the fellows told us that some of the "East End Boys" [13-17] "hang" at a candy store on Morgan near the Maxwell Police Station. After talking briefly to Mr. Carter [the Executive Secretary of that YMCA], we drove to the candy store. About 13 to 15 boys were there, including 6 "East End Boys" and one Mexican named George [16, last name not known] who is allegedly a leader of the "Jive Town" group. We talked to them about the same problem.

9:45 P.M.   E. Smith and I drove to HHBC-OP to meet 3 representatives of Boys Clubs of America in New York who are visiting Chicago specifically to learn more of CYDP. Fred Lickerman [Ass't. Executive Director of CBC], Frank Carney, AD, [the CYDP street-club work Supervisor] and John Ray [Outpost Supervisor] were also present. We discussed the project at length.

11:00 P.M.   Left for home.

Comment: I wrote a letter to Mr. Chorley [Director of CBC Camps] today confirming camping dates for next April 1-3 and April 29-May 1. I sent Mr. Kindler [OBC Director] a carbon copy.

*   *   *

THURSDAY

11:00 A.M.   I arrived at OBC and talked to the CYDP secretary about the typing of my reports. I then wrote yesterday's Daily Activity Report.

1:00 P.M.   I called Paul Mallory [Transo Envelope Co.] to confirm my meeting with him at 3:30 P.M. I am taking Allan Booker there to apply for one of the apprenticeship programs and for a tour of the facilities.

1:30 P.M.   Janie Banks [21] told me that a "friend of hers" has been contacted by a North Side man to push marijuana in this area.

3:00 P.M.   I picked up A. Booker and drove to 35XX N. Kimball Ave., Transo Envelope Co. While he filled out an application form, P. Mallory took me on a tour of the factory. P. Mallory then gave A. Booker the Wunderlick test and another test unknown to me. He scored 9 on the first, not good enough to be considered for the machine-adjuster program. P. Mallory hadn't scored the other test before we left. I was favorably impressed by the plant and their apprentice program (die-cutting, machine adjuster, and printing). A. Booker will be contacted later regarding Transo's decision.

6:00 P.M.   I drove A. Booker home and returned to OBC.

6:30 P.M.   Jimmy McMullan came to OBC and asked me to return the .32 automatic he gave me "to hold" on 11/16/65; he plans to sell it to a friend. Because a gun spells nothing but trouble, I told him I wouldn't return it. He accepted my decision. Marcia McMullan [17] came to OBC to talk to me about her husband. She is very unhappy—"I don't feel married." Apparently J. McMullan very seldom talks or spends an evening with her. Because she has so much time on her hands to brood—she is neither in school nor working— I encouraged her to become involved in some activities for her own sake; she mentioned the West Side Organization and I also suggested the Riis School Improvement Organization. She took about an hour getting all her concerns in the open. We discussed extensively the problems of married living, especially for young people.

8:00 P.M.   I talked briefly to Melvin Harris who is now working for Bud Shaffer [former OBC Board member] at the Merchandise Mart. He is working in an experimental lab and enjoys the work.

8:30 P.M.   Joe Martinez [former CYDP-CRC] came to OBC. We discussed "old times."

9:00 P.M.   I went to the Perkins residence, 8XX S. Lytle St., and talked to Mrs. Perkins and Mark Perkins [15]. Neither M. Perkins nor Carl Parkins [17] have been going to school; C. Perkins was barred earlier this week for excessive absences and M. Perkins hasn't been going "because I'm failing everything anyway." I told him that just sitting in class was more useful than going to Parental School, which could happen because of his age. He reluctantly agreed to "give it a try."

9:30 P.M.   I drove 3 "Spanish Squires" [14-16] home.
10:00 P.M.   I left for home.

*   *   *

FRIDAY

1:30 P.M.   I arrived at OBC and called Paul Mallory regarding Allan Booker. He said that he wouldn't be able to make a decision regarding his being hired until the middle of next week.

2:30 P.M.   Ron Wolsfeld, CRC, and I patrolled the Jackson School area. There were three or four squad cars in the area. On Polk Street near May, I talked to a member of the "Spanish Squires" who asked if the club could have regular meetings again. He reported that they have new members. When I asked, he said they are not from the area. I told him that I'm in favor of having meetings for the fellows in the area, that others are welcome to attend, but they must provide their own transportation. He smiled and said, "I thought that's what you would say!"

3:00 P.M.   We returned to OBC and I drafted a letter to a friend of mine, Larry Warren, assistant pastor of a Lutheran church in Rockford, Ill., who wrote to ask me if I would be willing to speak to the church's youth group about street work and delinquent youth in February. Charles Grass and Edward Wade [Illinois State Employment Services], who are from the Halsted Progress Center, came to OBC to introduce themselves and their program to Ezra Smith, EW, and I. They are interested in getting in touch with local youth. We said we would help them.

3:30 P.M.   Two "Town Apostles" [15-19] came to OBC. They are still interested in putting on a play. We discussed the possibility of meeting on Saturdays.

4:00 P.M.   I called Bill Hildreth [connected with Hull House Theater] to confirm 8 complimentary passes to the City Players' performance of *Becket* at 6XX W. Wellington.

5:00 P.M.   Jimmy McMullan stopped briefly at OBC to tell me that he and his wife, Marcia had a "good discussion" last evening. They have been having marital difficulties, difficulty communicating.

5:30 P.M.   Allan Booker called me; I informed him of my conversation with P. Mallory earlier.

6:00 P.M.   Edgar "Sonny" Washington [17] and Albert Hamilton [17] came to OBC. E. Washington is on the OBC-Neighborhood Youth Corps payroll, but hasn't reported for work in about a week; he has the impression that William Kindler [OBC Director] will not allow him to continue working here at OBC because Kindler referred him to another job prospect. I told him I would talk to Kindler. When I asked why his brother, Buddy [15], hasn't been going to school, he said he didn't know, but that the truant officer from Jackson School is threatening to send him to Parental School or Montefiore.

6:30 P.M.   I patrolled the area on foot. On Harrison Street I stopped at 12XX W., the former residence of the Wilson brothers, Oscar [16] and Oliver [16]. The building is now abandoned as are most buildings on the north side of Harrison St. At Polk Street and Laflin I talked to 6 "Naturals" [15-17]. I was surprised to find them on their old corner; they haven't "hung tight" since this summer. I was surprised to see Jose "Poppy" Garcia [17] who had been in the Job Corps in New Jersey. He said he got tired of it and withdrew through proper procedures: "The streets is where it is, man." He says he intends to return to night school. About three of the fellows were already high on glue and alcohol. After telling them I would stop by later in the evening, I stopped at Stu's [Ada and Taylor streets] and talked to Dan Young [16]. Two "Naturals" were also there—plus three younger "East End Boys" [13-17]. Kris Nievez [14] came in later and asked if there was any possibility of visiting Joe Adams [17] who is at the Job Corps Center, Battle Creek, Michigan. I told her I would find out what the rules are concerning visitation.

7:30 P.M.   I returned to OBC.

8:00 P.M.   One of the boys [16] from the neighborhood rushed into OBC and reported that "Stu is beating up Harry Banks [17]." Gary Calabrese [a Chicago policeman by day and part-time OBC staff member at night] and I drove in his car to Stu's Vienna Hot Dog Stand (Ada and Taylor streets). Approximately six boys [15-17] were standing in front of the place. Just as we asked if they knew where Banks was, one of them calmly said, "There he is, now." As we turned, he (Banks) stopped in the middle of Taylor St. and threw a brick at one of the huge windows in Stu's. It hit above the window and fell just behind us. Before he could throw another, G. Calabrese and I got to him. He did not fight back and finally dropped the other bricks he had in his hands. As we led him to the car, he was on the verge of tears, seething with anger. He kept repeating, "I got to get him back—he beat me, he beat me." On several occasions, we had to block his path to prevent his impulse to break away. He finally, but reluctantly, got into the car, but asked several times, "Why are we going to the Boys Club?" G. Calabrese did most of the talking in the car. When we got to OBC, Banks had calmed down considerably, but was still intent on "getting back at Stu." I presented the obvious alternatives—to go ahead and break out his windows, which would only hurt him; to forget it, which at the time was out of the question; or to use a "weapon" which is the right of a youth as well as an adult, namely *the law*. He decided he wanted to file a complaint. I called the police for him and was told that a car was already dispatched to Stu's. After a second call to the same number, four policemen arrived at OBC. Unfortunately, the rule rather than the exception prevailed. The police succeeded in doing little but increasing Banks' anger. When he related that Stu hit him first, one of the officers responded, "Don't give me that bullshit!" The senior officer softened somewhat and reminded Banks that it was his right to file a complaint if he so desired Monday (12/13/65) morning. When E. Smith, EW, came in, he took Banks aside. I joined them in a few moments. E. Smith assured him that if he decided to press charges, we supported him, but "if you want to get the man where it counts, hit him in the pockets—nobody buys hot dogs at Stu's." Jerry and Janir Banks [21] were also at the OBC. I told Jerry Banks [18] that if H. Banks still wanted to file a complaint on Monday, to be at OBC Monday morning at about 8:00 A.M. with his mother and one or two witnesses to the incident.

8:45 P.M.   Pauline S. (OBC staff) told me her daughter Marie [15] had just called to tell her that the "Jive Town" boys had already . learned of the incident and were waiting for "the word to turn out

Stu." She told her daughter about the boycott and to "cool it." H. Banks then left for home.

9:30 P.M. I patrolled the area. It was raining steadily which gave me cause to be alarmed about a group of about 15 Mexican youths standing on the sidewalk near 13XX W. Taylor St. After parking the car, I walked toward the gathering. From a distance I saw about four fellows pulling two others apart. Eight of those present were "Naturals" [15-17] and Gabe Lopez [16], a former "Barracuda" [15-17], John "Gorilla Joe" Cruz [17], a former "Natural," some girls, and a couple of neighborhood kids [15-16]. Six of the "Naturals" walked back toward Polk and Laflin sts. as Tommy "Bug" Rodriquez [16] and Albert Hamilton stopped to talk to G. Lopez and J. Cruz. Rafael Ramirez [16], who was drunk, had walked up to J. Cruz, flipped his necktie and slugged him in the mouth. Both T. Rodriquez and A. Hamilton asked the two to forget the incident, that R. Ramirez was blaming J. Cruz "for what happened to Joe Adams" [17—about two months ago G. Lopez blew his top: "It was me who kicked his ass—why doesn't he come after me!"]. I was afraid a fight would ensue because G. Lopez's remarks were very provoking, but both "Naturals" remained "cool" and left. J. Cruz continued to rant and rage: "You don't think I can do it; I can bring colored, spics, Italians, from Marshall and Crane high schools, all over—not by dozens, hundreds, but thousands, millions, and burn up this _ _ _ _ ing neighborhood. Next time I walk the streets, I'll have my uncle's gun, man!" Both began to cool down somewhat as I told them I'm sure they had the good sense not to mess themselves up by "dirtying your hands with fellows who still think it's big to stand on a corner drinking from a bottle." Mr. and Mrs. Lopez, Susan [18] and Dicky [14] Lopez were standing in the doorway, Mr. Lopez holding onto their German shepherd.

10:30 P.M. I continued to patrol the area. I saw T. Rodriquez [16] and A. Hamilton with their girlfriends going east on Taylor Street near Throop. T. Rodriquez said he talked to R. Ramirez who "will forget the whole thing."

11:00 P.M. I left the area.

* * *

SATURDAY

8:00 A.M.   I arrived at OBC to transport 3 "Spanish Squires" [14-16] to 71XX S. Coles St. to take a competitive examination for scholarships at an eastern prep school. Jesse Rivera [14] was the only one who didn't show up.

9:30 A.M.   I left the area after checking Stu's [Ada and Taylor streets], the location of an incident involving Stu and Harry Banks last evening. Since 11:00 P.M. last evening and 9:30 A.M. today, one of the windows was broken.

7:00 P.M.   I returned to the area and patrolled, just in case. There was nothing unusual going on.

8:00 P.M.   My date and I picked up Earl Young [18, CYDP Program Aide], his date, Jimmy McMullan and his wife Marcia, and drove to 6XX W. Wellington St. to attend the production of *Becket* for which I had complimentary passes.

11:30 P.M.   I drove everyone home and then patrolled the area. At Throop and Taylor Sts. I talked to Harry Banks and four friends [16-18].

12:00 N.   As I was leaving the area, I noticed that the Moreno family, 13XX W. Taylor St. was in the process of moving.

Comment: I wrote a letter to the Custer Job Corps Training Center at Battle Creek, Michigan today, in an attempt to arrange a visit to Joe Adams by six of his friends. I am afraid that if he is not given some moral support or dissuasion he might go AWOL and return to "the streets."

Bibliography

1. Frank Tannenbaun, *Crime and the Community*, Ginn and Co., Boston, 1938; reprinted by Columbia University Press, New York, N.Y., 1951 and 1957.

2. Richard A. Cloward and Lloyd E. Ohlin, *Delinquency and Opportunity*, The Free Press of Glencoe, Ill., 1960.

3. Albert K. Cohen, *Delinquent Boys*, The Free Press of Glencoe, Ill., 1955.

4. Frederick M. Thrasher, *The Gang*, The University of Chicago Press, Phoenix Edition, 1963.

5. Marvin E. Wolfgang, Leonard Savitz, and Norman Johnston (eds.), *The Sociology of Crime and Delinquency*, John Wiley and Sons, New York, N.Y., 1962.

6. Norman Johnston, Leonard Savitz and Marvin E. Wolfgang (eds.), *The Sociology of Punishment and Correction*, John Wiley and Sons, New York, N.Y., 1962.

7. U.S. Children's Bureau, *Juvenile Delinquency: Facts and Facets*, Nos. 1-18, Washington, D.C., 1960.

8. Martin Gold and J. Allan Winter, *A Selective Review of Community-Based Programs For Preventing Delinquency*, Institute for Social Research, The University of Michigan, Ann Arbor, Michigan (Children, Youth & Family Life series).

9. James F. Short Jr. and Fred L. Strodbeck, *Group Process and Gang Delinquency*, The University of Chicago Press, Chicago, Ill., 1966.

10. Oliver Moles, Ronald Lippitt and Stephen Withey, *A Selective Review of Research and Theory on Delinquency*, Institute for Social Research, The University of Michigan, Ann Arbor, Michigan (Children, Youth & Family Life series).

11. Irving Spergel, *Racketville, Slumtown and Haulberg*, The University of Chicago Press, Chicago, Ill., 1964.

12. Malcolm W. Klein and Barbara Myerhoff (eds.), *Juvenile Gangs in Context: Theory, Research and Action;* Conference Report: Youth Studies Center, University of Southern California, Los Angeles, Calif., 1963.

13. William Foote Whyte, *Street Corner Society: The Social Structure of an Italian Slum,* The University of Chicago Press, Chicago, Ill., Enl. 2nd ed., 1955.

14. Herbert J. Gans, *The Urban Villagers,* The Free Press of Glencoe, Ill., 1962.

15. David Matza, *Delinquency and Drift,* Wiley and Sons, New York, N.Y., 1964.

16. Anatol Rappaport, *Fights, Games and Debates,* The University of Michigan Press, Ann Arbor, Michigan, 1960.

17. Fritz Redl and David Wineman, *Children Who Hate,* The Free Press, Macmillan, N.Y., 1964.

18. Saul Bernstein, *Youth on the Streets,* Association Press, New York, N.Y., 1964.

19. Irving Spergel, *Street Gang Work: Theory and Practice,* Addison-Wesley Publishing Co., Inc., Reading, Mass., 1966.

20. Rose Giallombardo, (Ed.), *Juvenile Delinquency: A Book of Readings,* Wiley and Sons, New York, N.Y., 1966.

Bibliography Comments

General Readings

5. This is the finest collection of readings available to the student of crime and delinquency. Almost every article in the book should be read by anyone seriously interest in out-reach work.

6. This collection of readings is focused on the law and prison systems in general. Mandatory reading for the serious student of crime and delinquency.

7. These readings are somewhat dated but they provide background for more recent and advanced studies.

8. Indispensable reading for every worker. Thorough perusal of this volume will help the practitioner avoid many mistakes.

10. This is the best review and abstraction of all the important papers and books in the field of juvenile delinquency.

12. An advanced collection of important articles. This is very definitely for the advanced student.

Theoretical Works

1. A classic. Should be read by every worker, especially the first half of the book. The examples and illustrations may seem dated but this does not affect the work as a whole.

2. A very influential and stimulating work. The Mobilization for Youth Project in New York City is based upon the ideas put forth herein.

3. This work has become quite dated but it remains one of the important books for the student of crime and delinquency.

4. This should be read for its historical interest.

11. An attempt to "test out" some of Ohlin's and Cloward's formulations.

13. Mandatory reading for all workers even though it does not deal specifically with an antisocial gang group.

14. This should be read for the perspective it gives on the "inner-city" ethnic community. Although it deals specifically with an Italian community, much of what it has to say applies generally to the "inner city."

15. A most stimulating and ingenious interpretation of delinquency. It should be read by all workers.

16. Should be read by every worker. Part I is probably too technical for most readers, but Part II provides the reader with a way of looking at persuasion which is probably the best available.

17. Should be read for the perspective it gives on children who are characterized by their anger and hate. It is not necessary to be a Freudian to derive benefit from this book even though the perspective is psychoanalytical.